AUDREY MEISNER

like
yourself,
love your *life*

overcome big mistakes &
celebrate your true beauty

Like Yourself, Love Your Life:
Overcome Big Mistakes & Celebrate Your True Beauty

ISBN: 978-1-935870-01-2
UPC: 88571300071-0

Cover design by Yvonne Parks at www.pearcreative.ca
Cover photography by David Gauthier
Internal design by David Sluka

True Potential, Inc.
P.O. Box 904, Travelers Rest, SC 29690
www.tppress.com • 864.836.4111 • contact@tppress.com

Printed in the United States of America

dedication

To the most beautiful girl in the world:

You had me at first glance.
You won my heart and you will hold it forever.

Janelle Audrey Meisner

"…yes I love being here with you"

acknowledgements

I WOULD LIKE TO THANK my mom and dad. They have celebrated me and cheered me on every day of my life. They have taught me the indescribable joy that is found in loving people and celebrating Jesus. They have demonstrated a life of self-sacrifice and laughing through adversity. All of this, plus they are, without exception, the cutest parents in the world.

My husband Bob is my favorite person in the world, hands down. We do everything together and never tire of each other's company. We are crazy about each other and I adore him. I love being alone with him, I love traveling with him, I love parenting with him, and I love working with him. For some reason he's super sexy when he preaches because he's so good at it! I want to thank Bob for his part in this book. Not only has he forgiven me, but he trusts me implicitly and is passionate about communicating the message within these pages.

The journey to laughing easily with peace in my heart has not come without intention and instruction from my mentor, Dr. Jim Richards. I'd like to thank him for his years of study and wise perspective. Heart Physics® has brought me more freedom than I could have imagined. My favorite part about Jim is that we are family together, and Bob and I treasure our forever-friendship with him and Brenda.

On a practical note, my editor David Sluka has had the ability to hear beyond my words and capture my heart for women. His attention to detail amazes me, and I just plain old love working with him! I want to thank Yvonne from PearCreative who designed the cover and literally made me put my photo on the front cover (I really love her). And of course, David Gauthier who took the photograph. What a great team.

Thank you Jesus for the honor of speaking to women about love, acceptance, and forgiveness. I thrive in my secret place with you and there's nowhere I'd rather be. We harvest together, we rest in the garden, and you speak to me in ways that exceed my wildest dreams. We dream, rest, and laugh together and I can't wait to see you face to face.

Contents

You can tap into the irresistible beautiful girl you were created to be. All it takes is a single choice and then a commitment to journey to the place where you agree with how God feels about you.

I craved an escape. In desperation, I created a mess through trying too hard to get approval, busyness, and stuffing my feelings. In the middle of my mess I found hope and faced the irreversible consequences head on.

My self-inflicted tragedy could have been prevented. Initially the affair promised pleasure and escape. If only I would have known the truth: sin always results in pain. Oh, the true pleasure found in God's amazing grace.

foreword
by bob meisner

IF THERE'S ONE THING I DID RIGHT IN LIFE it was marrying Audrey. Since our first meeting in 1983 my life has been all the better for it. She is so much more than my wife or mother to our four children. She is my very, very best friend. So I am honored to introduce you to an exceptional woman who's deepest passion is to know the fullness of the depths and richness of God's love and to demonstrate that love to all those she meets.

Just the other morning I awoke while everyone in the house was still asleep. The glow of the morning sun slid its way through the blinds hung in the window next to our bed. I carefully rolled over and there, peacefully resting with her head on the pillow, was my Bride (of 26 years). I quickly resisted the immediate urge to touch, not wanting to wake her. As I watched, I smiled, and my heart overflowed with loving thoughts (I again reminded myself, don't touch!).

Then I had a new thought – *she loves her life*. With a gentle smile on her face she sleeps in peace and I see her as never before in complete rest with herself. I'm having a "wow moment." She lives life from a place of peace. I know in just a few moments she'll awake with a start, feet running before they hit the floor. But in this moment - I see the transformation... she's free.

Within these pages you will read stories of triumph, defeat, brokenness, healing, and laughter wrapped up in a whole lot of HOPE. Your future can be free from the limiting beliefs of a wounded past. You may have even found the title of this book a little offensive simply because you didn't realize you were even allowed to think this way, let alone live like this.

I encourage you to take this journey with Audrey. Allow her to become a friend who will help guide you as you take the steps needed to discover your life of wholeness. In this life God has for you, there are generous amounts of joy for each day. And even if your day is exhausting, you will have found the Prince of Peace and your sleep will be sweet.

Within your hands you hold a dream turned reality. It's not a book, but rather a glimpse into a life transformed. Maybe you're like Audrey who thought her life had spiraled out of control with no hope of a happy landing. Or maybe you're one who has given-up, resigned to believe that uninhibited laughter is reserved only for children or those who don't take life serious enough. If so, then this is your day of new beginnings.

We each have "articles" in our lives that we tend to carry around with us far too long. The Bible calls them "weights." These are the non-essentials that slow us down. They're not always sins. Often they are beliefs in our hearts and stuff that clutters our lives that we have grown so accustomed to. We have placed such importance upon them believing they are what define us and have kept us stable all these years. I'll agree they had a purpose for a season, but can we begin to trust yet again that there is celebration awaiting us? Beyond living in a survival mode or simply maintaining stability, there is an invitation given by the King of kings. This grace is extended to you, capable of escorting you through personal victory where you may enter into the dance once again. Your life has a preferred future of significance where you are to influence others with the song of your heart, invoking them to discover their dance with the King.

My prayer for you is that you will reconnect with God. Our music and worship services help us to exalt the Lord, but have they led us to experience Him? Enduring hardship is directly related to having an enduring vision. An enduring vision is one that is rooted deep in the heart. It's the unshakeable certainty that the end is sure. We must experience something that influences our hearts greater than our hardship. I'm asking you to begin trusting again. Trust is a great emotion. Your heavenly Father has never stopped working behind the scenes of your life. You may be missing His preserved presence, but pause long enough to hear His voice speaking, "I trust you." Move in His direction. There may be wounds needing to be healed, and this book will help you to heal, but more importantly there is a victory dance to be celebrated.

I am so grateful Audrey never quit on me and even more thankful that she has found her dance!

chapter 1

stop beating yourself up

You can tap into the irresistible beautiful girl you
were created to be. All it takes is a single choice and
then a commitment to journey to the place where
you agree with how God feels about you.

Do you recognize how hard you are on yourself?

Have you considered how many debilitating thoughts bombard you each day? You're not alone. Many of us are beating ourselves up, and it must stop. Instead of wasting our energy on the fight within our hearts, it is time to come to terms with our past, know who we really are, and embrace where we're headed so that we can learn to love ourselves and each other. This is an exciting journey we get to take together. This is a divine appointment!

To say I've messed up is an understatement. I clearly remember the feeling of utter hopelessness and shame as I walked out of the doctor's office in the winter of 2001. The test confirmed that I was pregnant. It was only two weeks prior that I gathered every ounce of courage I had and confessed to my husband that I had betrayed him. I had sex with another man and the baby wouldn't look anything like our other three kids. My picture perfect life was about to crash and burn. My foolish, selfish choices were about to bring chaos and death to any future of having a happy family. And it was completely my fault!

Fast-forward to today. My marriage and family have been rescued. I have forgiven myself. Yes, I deserved punishment, torment, and life-long consequences. I should be carrying around extraordinary amounts of shame while exerting lots of energy trying to cover up my past. Instead I am living life—loved—and loving the life I live. I have a tremendous amount of peace in my heart with no fear of the future.

How did I get from the place of despair to actually celebrating my existence? It didn't happen instantly, and along the journey I discovered some secrets to loving life. I'm exploding with anticipation as I share these with you because if there is hope for me, there is hope for you.

What it Means to Like Yourself

Early this morning my husband Bob was complimenting me. In my barely-awake daze I could tell that he was cherishing everything about me. He loved my soft skin and was enamored by my womanly beauty. His words were sincere as he said, "You're sexy." I smiled and softly said, "That's because you like me."

A few years ago, I would have probably would have dismissed him and said, "Seriously? Me? Sexy? I don't think so. But now I am starting to understand the power of "like." Bob likes me and I really like him. When you like someone, you enjoy them. You notice the qualities of their personality that are attractive. You admire the beauty they emanate. Even though you are aware they aren't perfect and see their flaws and weaknesses, you don't really care. You're not overlooking them; you just like them too much to think about that! You are choosing to minimize the unlovely because your heart is too busy enjoying the benefits of being together.

I'm just like most other women. I have some pretty obvious physical flaws, lumps, rolls, and unattractive dimples. I don't have a perfectly toned body, and I don't especially like seeing myself naked in a mirror. However, instead of rejecting Bob's comment, I received his sincere and loving compliments. He likes me! Instead of thinking of my negative imperfections, he was soaking up the soft and smooth touch of his wife's skin.

There's a lot of power in liking someone. You crave time with that person and enjoy the chemistry of the relationship and the animated conversation it creates. Can you imagine that kind of relationship with yourself? Can you imagine that kind of relationship with God?

Since I was a very little girl, I knew that God loved me. However, I've spent the rest of my life discovering that Jesus *likes* me. That means He enjoys me. And I definitely like Him back. If He likes me, then in order to be in agreement with Him, I need to like myself too.

Choosing to like myself has been a challenge. I'm energetic and loud, so you can't miss me. I used to apologize for my personality and even attempt to hone it in hopes to be more acceptable in a "society" kind of way. But it's never fun to pretend you're someone else, and it's impossible to feel normal – because there's no such thing! Every single one of us is uniquely amazing. I've come to this conclusion after spending much time alone with God and asking His opinion. During these times I have discovered a treasure I never thought possible: A completely safe, not-one-bit-fake relationship with my invisible God that has proved Himself to be more real than the chair I'm sitting on.

It's never fun to pretend you're someone else, and it's impossible to feel normal – because there's no such thing!

The result of this electric-relationship we have together is that we share secrets, we smile a lot, we crave time alone together, and we get to spend eternity together. While He *is* perfect and flawless, He doesn't focus on my shortcomings. He knows everything about me – and I mean everything – and has this amazing ability to like me even when I fail.

So here's where I'm at now. Please believe me, it has been a journey, but I'm in a new place. I like hanging out with myself. I laugh at funny thoughts, cheery memories, and animated ideas that run through my head. I have forgiven myself because God has assured me that I am forgiven. I'm at peace with the thoughts in my head so I don't over-analyze and beat myself up anymore. I'm childlike because I have tapped into a radical trust in my heavenly Father. I love letting the moment explode with unbridled enthusiasm for life. Oh, and you *know* I dance like nobody's watching. Mostly only when nobody is watching of course.

No matter your age, your shape, your size, your personality type, or the present circumstance you find yourself in, you want to be happy and you can be. Happy people are contagious. They usually love what they do and their joy is refreshing. We can't afford to analyze what others think. We must, without restraint, dive into the life we were meant to live.

Learning to Love

As you read this book, I consider it an intimate time we have together. When we're together, I want to see the full-on unbridled expression of who God really created you to be. I want the absolute best for you – and I definitely want you happy. Let's embark on a journey to love yourself, and like yourself too!

There's no time like the present – and believe me, being nice to yourself IS going to feel like a present! The days of beating yourself up for no apparent reason are officially over. Besides, that self-defeating behavior leaves you bruised and bleeding (hypothetically, of course). No one looks good or feels good when they're trying too hard and getting nowhere.

You are about to see yourself the way God sees you. Your gorgeous self is possibly locked deep inside of you, and I am going to thoroughly enjoy taking a wrecking ball to walls of unprecedented guilt, heavy self-inflicted shame, and habitual, negative self-talk. Why don't you take a deep breath right now and whisper your intent, "I'm ready to love life again."

You may think your life is complicated, but thankfully the solutions to life are refreshingly simple. Remember the acronym: K-I-S-S? "Keep-It-Simple-Stupid." Well, I would never call you or me or even someone I don't like "stupid" so let's replace that with *silly*. In other words, "Silly me! I have allowed lack of love, money, and energy to zap my beauty and rob me of loving life. I have allowed the disappointments in life to build a hard-shell around my heart. I have regressed into a downward spiral of overwhelming circumstances and I've forgotten the root of all things wonderful, which is love." It's that simple.

The Beatles were pretty edgy-crazy in their philosophy of life, but they definitely got the words right when they sang *All We Need Is Love*. But we don't want to just get the words right, we want to get our hearts right to agree with God's idea of what love is. Getting words right won't change your life.

There's a chapter in the Bible that's all about love and concludes:

> Three things will last forever—faith, hope, and love—and the greatest of these is love.[1]

God's love transcends the human definition of love to a point that is hard for" us to comprehend. But I want to spend my life searching out the treasure of His love, for He just doesn't "do" love, He "is" love.

Do you want to be happy, successful, and fulfilled in every area of life? Do you want to have peace in your heart and purpose for each day? Know love. This journey we are on will take us to depths of discovering his love.

> And may you have the power to understand as all God's people should, how wide, how long, how high and how deep His love is. May you experience the love of Christ, though it is too great to understand fully. Then you will be made complete, with all the fullness of life and power that comes from God.[2]

To know Him is to love Him. In my own experience, as I have come to know Him, I love him more and more. Even though I have failed, He continues to love me to life. This is literally the secret to loving life: Love the Lord your God with all your heart, soul, mind and strength and love others as you love yourself.[3]

It's that simple, but it's not always easy. Unfortunately, hurting people have hurt us – sometimes on purpose, sometimes by accident. We then often draw negative conclusions and write wrong judgments on our hearts, which then forms unhealthy thought patterns. Our life experiences create filters in which we begin to believe lies about ourselves, others, and even God.

No one is immune; we all have experienced pain, shame, embarrassment, rejection, fear, and anger. Disappointment and disaster has had opportunity to slam our lives. The residue of these emotions and experiences leaves us feeling like our hearts are broken and confused.

So how does love solve *every single problem* we encounter? Every positive emotion you feel is rooted in love. On the contrary, every negative emotion you feel is rooted in fear. Logic attempts to persuade us that *power* will overcome *fear*. Therefore, *I must be stronger, more confident, more determined, and more resilient. Somehow, I WILL overpower the fear that abides in my heart.* Even though this response appears logical, it doesn't work. Power does not overcome fear.

How then do we rid our heart of fear – if that truly is the root of every negative emotion? If power and a strong will won't do it, what will? I love the Bible – it has an answer for these extremely pertinent questions! It says that "perfect love expels all fear."[4]

There's only one place to get perfect love – and that's from God. He's the only one who is completely perfect, who wants to benefit your life in every way, and cherishes and adores you – even when you screw up. Not only that, but He created you. That means He knows you even better than you know yourself. He knows your thoughts, He knows your heart, and He wants to walk and talk with you through life.[5]

That's the best news! You aren't alone, and you don't have to figure out life all by yourself.

I guess that's the best news – you aren't alone, and you don't have to figure out life all by yourself. God is pursuing you and isn't hiding truth from you, but rather is waiting to deposit His wisdom and solutions. He definitely isn't disappointed in you, thinking of ways to punish you. He loves you with an extravagant, eternal, and unconditional love as your perfect father.

I have found that I love God and others best when I love myself and know I'm lovable. I also find that I can't love myself unless I let God love me. So it all starts with you being willing to *receive* God's love more than you ever have before. It pretty much goes in that order: Let God love you; you love yourself; you can love God; you can love others.

Becoming an expert on love makes you an expert on life. Pursuing the treasure of receiving and giving love will set you up to gain everything out of life that you possibly can, and fulfill the very purpose for which you were born.

About You

Alongside this book, I'd like to encourage you to assign a notebook, journal, or even a document in your computer to apply what you read to your life. There are also some extra journal pages at the back of this book. At the end of each chapter, and sometimes after sections within a chapter, there will be questions and a meditation to think about, answer, and act upon. There are no right or wrong answers – simply be willing to explore the deep places in your heart and pursue honest dialogue with God.

So turn the page and begin your journey toward liking yourself, and loving your life!

about you

- Do you recognize negative thoughts you tell yourself? Explain.

- How would you rate yourself on a scale of 1-10, where 10 is you like yourself completely and 1 is you do not like yourself at all?

- What are your fears, concerns, or obstacles when it comes to liking yourself?

- Open your heart to God loving you more than you ever have before. In your own words, invite Him to love you.

meditation

In the early 1990s I wrote and hosted a television show for kids with puppets and music. I composed more than forty songs for children during that time. I consider it one of the most privileged opportunities I have ever had to influence tender hearts to receive God's love. Children receive love without question. My hope for you is that like a child, you will receive God's extravagant and unconditional love.

Read an excerpt from a song I wrote, from the lips of a child:

You made the grass on the ground so green…
like a carpet for me

Telling me… You'll take good care of me

You made the sun moon and stars in the sky –
fluffy clouds flying by

Telling me… Your love is so high

I think of all that You've made,
and my heart is amazed

You're so big and I'm so small

Still You take time to love me…

Lord, You're thinking of me.

That's the greatest miracle of all

chapter 2

the set up for shame

I craved an escape. In desperation, I created a
mess through trying too hard to get approval,
busyness, and stuffing my feelings. In the
middle of my mess I found hope and faced
the irreversible consequences head on.

KNOWING I'M FORGIVEN has been the secret key to
forgiving myself. There was no excuse for what I did, and as a
result, I could have cowered into a depressed state for the rest
of my life. Instead…I discovered love.

Bob and I got married young in 1984. We both love people
and our goals reflected this as we pursued helping others in
need full time. Three kids were born by the time I was twenty-
six years old and we were crazy about them. Fast-forward seventeen years. The kids were fifteen, twelve, and ten years old,

extra people are living with us and we're super busy doing good things.

Bob and I worked together in my parent's television ministry. I was host of a daily news-magazine television show and we pastored a church together as well. I wasn't angry at anyone and I enjoyed our family and friends. I had a strong moral upbringing and came from an exceptionally happy family. God was extremely important to me, and I would describe our relationship together as daily, real, and growing.

Performance for Approval

So how does someone like this get into so much trouble? I see it like this. I spent my entire life learning the art of performance and always choosing to do the right thing. When Bob and I first got married, there were times that he disappointed me and even scared me.

Instead of confronting him, nagging him, or communicating my frustration, I would simply deal with it internally and choose to "forgive" him. Meanwhile, he never knew what I was going through and the growth of our relationship was stunted by my fear of confrontation. This dishonest behavior multiplied by seventeen years of marriage set me up for some deep-seeded resentment.

Busyness

Our lifestyle at the time of the affair was filled with busyness and generosity. We had chosen to pioneer a church that, at the beginning, brought excitement, energy, and purpose to our already busy lives. We volunteered not only hours upon hours of our time, but spent a startling amount of creative passion in hopes of growing a huge work for God. Over the years, people were disappointed and I took this very personally. I didn't see the growth I was hoping for and I condemned myself that I wasn't doing enough, or I wasn't good enough, smart enough, or gifted enough. I was disappointed in God, wondering why He didn't deem us worthy to make us more successful.

The weekly grind of church services, in additional to our full-time jobs and parenting our three children exhausted me. I prepared food, vacuumed the building before and after services, set up equipment, made sure the children's program was on task, and took leadership of the music.

I prayed for hours at a time, loved everyone who walked in the door to the best of my ability, and had a huge smile on my face. I didn't complain and I refused to cower to self-pity. After the Sunday service, when I finally got to bed, I would begin dreading that I had to do the whole thing again in seven days.

I was overwhelmed and exhausted. I was pouring out, giving to everyone who needed anything, and there was nothing left. I didn't like my life and felt lonely and misunderstood. Bob loved the church, so I couldn't bear to tell him how much I hated our lifestyle.

There was no way to "quit" a church, so I felt trapped and confused. I beat myself up, telling myself to grow up and be happy. I mean, aren't "unselfish" people the happiest people on earth? If anyone was being unselfish, it was me!

Stuffing the Feelings

I stuffed all feelings of resentment and chose to continue to give. I thought I was doing the right thing. But just as I wasn't honest with Bob about my true feelings, I wasn't even truthful to myself. Even writing this ten years later, I am coming to terms with my true feelings, but never would have been able to articulate them at the time.

I stuffed all feelings of resentment and chose to continue to give. I thought I was doing the right thing.

Performance was my specialty. I looked so good to everyone – even myself. So giving. So loving. So empty.

The truth was this emptiness in my heart was thirsting for refreshment in my life. I craved time for just me. I was so tired of doing the right thing and being so dang responsible. Inside I was screaming for attention. I ignored my needs and stuffed the desperation. I even punished myself with self-condemning thoughts.

Does all of this sound like a set up?

It was during this time that someone walked into my life. He had a broken heart and wanted fun, and so did I. We were like magnets to each other. With mutual brokenness we began to feed off of each other. This person made me laugh and feel like a kid again. When I was with him I felt irresponsible and silly. He respected me, appeared amazed by my noble and giving lifestyle, and was intrigued by my personality. This made me feel valuable and irresistible. He complimented me for my beauty and desired to be close to me. And to top it all off, being alone with him was forbidden, and this heightened my sense of adventure and risk.

Describing this to James Robison on *Life Today*, his television show, he responded to me, "There is a lot of powerful desire linked to the feeling of being wanted." Before I knew it, I thought about him constantly.

Deception Began

My perceived unselfish thoughts flipped and I began justifying my thoughts. I have the right to be happy. I have the right to have some time to myself. I have the right to hang out with someone who adores me. I give so much, I have the right to feel good and be happy.

Ironically, I had observed the unhappiness of people who are selfish and self-centered, and who ignore the needs of those around them. Yet, in attempts to be unselfish in every way, I ignored my own needs and set myself up for an expression of the epitome of selfishness – a sexual affair. The answer to my selfishness was love. But love rejoices in the truth, and truth was something I wasn't willing to face. I needed help and nobody knew my secret.

The Selfish Choice

This particular guy in our church started pursuing me and flirting with me. Initially I shrugged him off and never told Bob about it. After several months, I began to entertain the thoughts that were beginning to entice my heart, generating emotions. These intense emotions left unchecked eventually demanded action – actions that would lead to a behavior that completely contradicted my character and who I am.

I began to feel alive and beautiful again. Not that I wasn't loved by my husband, my children, and my church family, rather there was something broken in me that was looking for an escape to medicate the perceived pain of my heart. I believed I could control this and have both.

The friendship turned sexual and I found myself somewhere I never thought even possible – in a full-fledged affair. I loved my husband and kids. This selfish choice went against everything I believed. I quickly ended the relationship and confessed my infidelity to my husband, Bob. The repercussions of pain for both of us were excruciating.

Two weeks later we discovered the news that I had become pregnant during the affair. Hopelessness and despair overshadowed me. When I told Bob about the affair initially, I believed that we could get the help we needed and nobody would ever know about it. Now my secret would be obvious for the world to see. These depths of despair resulted in hopelessness, and because of my hopelessness, I was tempted to take matters into my own hands, thinking abortion would be the answer.

I know what it feels like to be in so much despair that there is no hope of a happy ending. Desperate people do shocking things. *Am I going to continue on this path of selfish preservation? Or am I going to scream out for help and find someone to speak truth into my life that will interrupt my thought patterns of destruction?* I considered an abortion, realizing that I would be known for the rest of my life by the most stupid and selfish thing I had ever done. Knowing abortion wasn't the answer, I desperately begged God for a miscarriage.

Even though my husband struggled through his own fears of inadequacy to love, he never left me. Together we sought outside counsel to rescue our relationship. Throughout the pregnancy I went through feelings of extreme fear of the future, fear of "Will I ever be able to feel God's presence again?" and "Will I ever be able to experience the safety and embrace of Bob's love?"

Hope for the Future

Both of us were extremely scared of what our future would hold as we went to the hospital to deliver the baby. But something beyond our imagination happened the moment *our* little baby was born. It was as if every ounce of fear drained from our imagination and peace overshadowed our family. Love freely flowed when our eyes met this perfect gift…our son. My husband gave the baby boy his own name, vowing that he never wants his "Robert" to ever wonder a day in his life who his daddy is.

The journey of forgiveness came in layers. It wasn't instantaneous, and Bob will tell you himself that he pushed me away and punished me for a period of time. But God captured his heart and loved him, and then he was able to love me. When I look back in retrospect, what Bob did to love me makes him my hero. Instead of continuing to punish me for my past mistakes, he rescued me as love rescued him.

With the shadows of the unknown revealed, we weathered the storm of the previous eight months and began to have glimmers of hope for the future.

Freedom Through Forgiveness

Even though Bob and I had worked through layers of forgiveness, it wasn't until years later that I began to realize I hadn't forgiven myself. As a leader in television and churches, the general public knew who I was, and I could feel the shame of people judging me and labeling me as a woman who didn't deserve anything good to happen to her. I agreed with them. My selfish betrayal caused excruciating pain to others and myself, and it never should have happened.

Instead of being a victim, labeled and ashamed, I was transformed into a person who can help others understand that their mistakes do not define them.

I thank God that one night I came to terms with the grief locked inside of me and I agreed to see myself as beautiful, loving, and forgiven. My life has totally changed since that moment. Instead of being a victim, labeled and ashamed, I was transformed into a person who can help others understand that their mistakes do not define them.

Knowing that I'm forgiven has been the secret key to being able to forgive myself.[6] There was no excuse for what I did, and as a result, I could have cowered into a depressed state for the rest of my life. Instead, I discovered love.

So many women live everyday life with thoughts of regrets, wrong choices, and life-altering mistakes. I have now committed my life to help women find the courage and faith to move beyond their past and embrace a new future of laughing and dreaming again. Every person, no matter who they are, has the opportunity to love life and be free to love herself.

I want to encourage you to invest a few minutes right now to go through the About You section on the next page. In a few chapters I'll talk about steps to forgiveness. For now, just know that you have a beautiful story to tell. You were created as a gift to this world. The choices you make to accept yourself, love yourself, and forgive yourself will pave the way to enjoy life to its fullest and find your smile once again.

about you

- Would you consider your lifestyle too busy? If so, what can you change?

- Do you ever find yourself craving escape? If so, what parts of your life don't you like? How can you change it without running from responsibility?

- Are you honest with yourself or do you stuff your feelings?

- Describe who you are in your "dream state" (i.e. full of joy, peaceful, forgiven, etc.).

meditation

No matter how busy or stressed you are or how noisy your surroundings may be, determine to get to a quiet place (even if you have to go to the bathroom and lock the door). Now close your eyes and slow down your thoughts. Meditate on what you look like and feel like completely free: Smiling; convinced that you're forgiven; persuaded that you are loved. Let yourself enjoy the emotions of how it feels. That's how God sees you.

chapter 3

∞

Tragedy Prevention

My self-inflicted tragedy could have been prevented.
Initially the affair promised pleasure and escape.
If only I would have known the truth: sin
always results in pain. Oh, the true pleasure
found in God's amazing grace.

COULD SOME OF THE UNFORTUNATE EVENTS of my past have been prevented? Absolutely. I now recognize the importance of being true to yourself and to your feelings. Even though feelings aren't always based on truth, they are very real in the moment. Ignoring your desperate need for fun, laughing, dreaming, and refreshment is almost like silently and slowly committing suicide.

Was pastoring the church wrong? Not at all. The church is supposed to be a beautiful expression of God on the earth!

Bob and I, our children, and countless others have cherished memories experiencing the magnitude of God's presence while we were pastoring. In fact, one could say that the sudden interruption of my affair, which caused this church to shut down, was an atrocity to what God was doing in many people's lives. The church was thriving.

The activities themselves were not the problem. The mistake was made when I didn't clearly identify the emptiness of my heart, be truthful with my needs and then communicate them to my husband. In the affair, I found someone who was willing to meet the lack I kept in the hidden corners of my heart. Had I been truthful, Bob would have willingly and joyfully made any sacrifice to bring priority and order to our lives. And the crisis need never have taken place.

The following are five actions that could have helped to prevent my tragedy.

God Must Be Your Source

I now recognize that God wants to meet every single desire of my heart. Bob will never be able to read my mind, be the perfect Prince Charming, and understand my feelings every moment. He's pretty amazing, but he's Bob, not God! As soon as we put expectation on any person to be our source – spouse, parents, children, friends, or spiritual leader – we are in a form of dysfunction where we develop co-dependent relationships. No matter how perfect the relationship begins, there will always be places of disappointment. These precious relationships can add to our fulfillment, but never, never can another person be our source.

We are designed for relationship, so even when disappointment is real, God never disappoints. It's hard to imagine that a holy God would understand my craziness and want to relate to me on such a personal level. I can trust Him to provide my needs, protect me, promote me, and love me perfectly. He has already approved of me, so I don't have to perform. He has assured me of my worth and identity as His daughter, so I don't have to try hard to earn His acceptance. He sets me up for laughter and fun, and the relationship we share is mutual as we delight and enjoy each other.

A holy God understands your craziness and wants to relate to you on a personal level. He has already approved of you so you don't have to perform.

I used to apologize for being silly and having fun until I embraced the fact that God made me like this and enjoys my personality! We don't just have serious, quiet times of Bible reading and prayer. Those times are extremely important and precious to me, but it doesn't stop there. We hang out together all day. I laugh at funny things, capture the enchanted beauty of the sunset, rest in the carefree breeze at night, and through it all I receive the inherent wisdom that He deposits into my heart. By *wisdom* I mean that I'm seeing life through His perspective.

My relationship with God was already a lot like this before the affair, but through the pain of the crisis that we endured, I learned to love God's perspective. That's what's different about me after the affair. I hate sin and I love truth. Jesus was not kidding when He said, "And you will know the truth, and the truth will set you free."[7] My fear of disappointing people paralyzed me from telling the truth. My fear of failure forced me to perform and be perfect. I had no idea that these fears could affect nearly twenty years of marriage.

Drop the Pride and Think Straight

The kicker-question is, *How could I have become deceived enough to go through with such obvious sin?* That is the power of deception. We are susceptible to believe a lie when pride is in our heart. I didn't think I was capable of such a sin. Pride is the reason why I could be friends with this young guy and spend time alone with him. In essence, I was saying, "I don't really need God." My pride was actually causing resistance in my relationship with Him.[8] I was in control of this relationship and was clearly not thinking of myself the way I should.[9] I didn't commit adultery overnight.

Slowly, my heart became hardened as I assumed control of my own life. I began to compartmentalize my thoughts and feelings. I wanted God to be involved in my life in some areas, but I closed him off where I was justifying, rationalizing, and believing I could get what I needed from this inappropriate relationship. I actually thought I was in complete control and could stop at any time. I controlled it for a short while, but within time it controlled me and I became a slave to the cravings it had created in me. I made a series of compromises over many months that resulted in my life being like a Ferris wheel out of control. I couldn't get off.

What was once exhilarating, risky, thrilling, and forbidden was now like a drug with its extreme highs that would throw me to the ground in a low where I hated my life. Today it is sickening to me to think that I enjoyed that warped pleasure that sin brings only for a season. The most deadly lie was that I could manage my marriage and ministry while participating in something that was obviously wrong. That's why I'm writing to you. I don't want you to be enslaved as I was or desperate for escape. Don't let circumstances determine your life. You can find truth, and Jesus has grace enough to take you through.

Every habit, addiction, or destructive behavior comes from the belief that you will benefit from that activity. It could provide pleasure, escape, or relief. The truth is that every sin only leads to pain. Oh yes, it looks like and even feels like pleasure for a season, but the sin will never satisfy.

Every habit, addiction, or destructive behavior comes from the belief that you will benefit from that activity. The truth is that every sin only leads to pain.

I continued in my behavior for a few weeks thinking I was seeking happiness, pleasure, and thrill. Meanwhile, I was confused, an emotional wreck, and acting like an immature, self-centered crazy-person. I lied to the people I loved the most in order to chisel in time to see this person. I couldn't sleep at night, lying awake wondering what had led me to actually have an affair.

In retrospect, some of the lies I believed were illogical and pretty much insane. In the moment, they all made sense to me. I have seen these subtle lies seep into many who thought they were immune. At first, I thought I could enjoy friendship with him without it getting sexual. I wasn't physically attracted to him initially and he was much younger than me. I thought I could still have and love my husband and kids, and just have this guy as an extra boyfriend. I believed this guy met needs in my life and nobody would ever have to know.

I know for a fact that many people relate to these thoughts and have been tricked into the same illicit type of relationship that I was. After the relationship began, it was like a drug, an addiction, and I needed my fix.

It is my hope for anyone still involved in an affair that they will look at the big picture and face the reality that this relationship will bring only destruction and pain. People won't be convinced to end a relationship they are thoroughly enjoying in the moment, even if it is wrong. Every person will do what he or she wants to do. However, I will show you later how to explore the possibility of new, healthy desires so that you can experience wisdom and life transformation during temptation.

After breaking off any form of contact with this man, I faced many painful situations. I continued to live with Bob who was extremely angry with me (justifiably so), but I pretended to be okay while my entire life was falling apart. I lived, breathed, and was consumed with guilt for what I had done.

When I found out I was pregnant, I didn't think I could face my life. My mind was consumed with fear and shame:

I'm going to be known forever by the most stupid and selfish thing I have ever done. My kids are going to be messed up. I call myself a "Jesus Girl" and now I'm disqualified from ever speaking about my faith and love for God.

My tendency towards performance went into overload. I obeyed precisely every instruction that was given to me. If I was told to keep my secret quiet, even from my best friend, I obeyed. The tormenting thoughts of guilt and shame demanded punishment. Bob was so devastated at what I had done that he would recoil in pain and lash out with anger and rage and rejection. He would interrogate me yet again with questions about what I had done. Understandably so, he could not resolve why I had done what I did. I believed I deserved all the punishment that came my way. I resolved to have no will of my own, and didn't think I deserved to make any decisions.

I couldn't feel God's presence. I was numb emotionally. I had to wear a mask to live life as a mom, a TV host, and a friend. Nobody knew what was going on beneath the surface. I was barely surviving. I knew that God was with me, so out of faith I talked to Him, mostly just asking him to please help me to live another day. *Please take this baby. I can't handle it. Please help Bob to forgive me.*

Talk to God and Let Him Carry You

In hindsight I can clearly recognize God's amazing grace to me during this season of my life. He never left me. He cried with me. He heard every one of my prayers. He didn't answer them the way I thought He should, and definitely not as quickly as I thought I needed him to. But He loved me and held my hand as we lived through each day. Sometimes it would feel like two hours had passed and it was only ten minutes. It's as if pain makes time stand still.

We quit our jobs, moved, and got established in Phoenix, Arizona, where we were receiving help and love from our new church family. We had good days and bad days, but the pastor that was helping us refused to let us feel sorry for ourselves. He encouraged us to rather embrace the reality and truth of the situation and find God's grace for every moment.

I ignored the fact that I was pregnant and worked my fingers to the bone. In order to be perfect in attempts to earn Bob's love back, I cleaned the house, took care of the kids, and rode my bicycle to get groceries or visit the library to get an Internet connection. We didn't have telephones or most modern conveniences. We lived on very little money and I stretched our dollar by careful grocery shopping. Going to bed was always the hardest for me. I would be physically and emotionally spent and Bob often wanted to talk about "it." He would ask me why I did it. At the time I didn't understand or have a clue why I did it. I was as confused as he was. He asked me difficult questions I couldn't answer, so I usually just cried. Agony and a deep pit in my stomach was what I usually felt as I faced the night. I longed to feel safe with Bob and find true rest and a peaceful night's sleep.

One night after Bob let me go to sleep, I remember rolling over with my head on the pillow, talking silently to God. I was about five months pregnant. I hadn't written out my conversations with God for months since I found out that Bob had been reading my journal and was hurt by my confusion. So even though journaling was a big part of my daily relationship with God for years and an outlet for honesty and prayer, I had quit completely.

On this night, I tried to cry quietly, but poured out my heart to God. I asked Him, "When will I journal again? When will I get to be alone with You and You listen to me as I write out my prayers? When will I hear Your answers and write out your precious words to me…" I just didn't have enough strength, faith, or courage to write. I drifted off to sleep.

The next morning, I woke up, fulfilled all my daily morning activities, said goodbye to Bob as he left for work, and walked towards the front door. There was a bag on the doorknob. It was from a bookstore and inside was a beautiful journal with the words, "The Lord is my Shepherd."

Nobody but God knew the cry of my heart the night before. He whispered to one of my new friends in Phoenix to buy me a journal and put it on my door. She had no clue what I was going through. I wept and wept as I felt God's love. *He cares about me! He wants me to journal again! I can tell Him about the details of my life, and He can heal my broken heart.*

I sat down and began to write and write and write. I am always very honest with God about my feelings and my questions, and then I write out Bible verses that He leads me to. This day I wrote:

> Lord, You are my shepherd. You lead me to still
> waters. You lead me to green pastures. You restore
> my soul. Even though I walk through the valley of

the shadow of death, I know You are with me. Your rod and Your staff, they comfort me.[10]

It was as if I drank in His love, peace, and the reality of His presence. I asked Him, "Lord, why is it that for my first three pregnancies, I was deathly-sick-nauseated every day of the nine months and had to spend each day surviving on the couch – and yet with this pregnancy I haven't even been sick even one day?"

God replied to me, "Audrey, you haven't had the strength to carry this baby. I'm carrying him for you." That's exactly how it felt. I didn't feel the ramifications of pregnancy even though I was five months along. God's grace and mercy carried me and the baby as we walked through the painful journey towards heart healing. From that day on, I talked with God in detail in my journal and began receiving God's wisdom and perspective.

Receive God's Amazing Grace

As far as our marriage relationship, we were determined to stay together. It was not easy to be together. Bob would be nice to me sometimes, and I remember feeling so grateful. But I also knew that things were fragile. Our pastor challenged Bob to stop asking *why* and start asking *what now*. Another counselor friend of ours asked Bob, "When are you going to stop punishing her?" He replied, "I'm not punishing her! I've stayed with her and I'm not leaving the family…," to which she replied, "Yes you are punishing her by withholding affection from her." She asked Bob when he planned on stopping the conversations about the incident. As long as he continued to make it a focal point, he would prolong the healing process.

My pastor challenged me when asking, "When did you stop respecting Bob?" I gave him a puzzled look and evaluated my life. I believe I preferred him, served him without complaining, and was a great co-worker in the church that we led together. But no wife can betray her husband and still have respect; it just doesn't happen. I never felt like the affair was *against* Bob. It was more about having an *extra relationship*, an addition. I had to take a hard look at my heart motives and begin identifying the thoughts and ways I had lost respect for Bob. I appreciate the fact that my pastor constantly challenged both Bob and I and refused to be our answer. He always influenced us towards finding God's grace, character, and nature and embracing His answers.

Our journey continued and our pain continued, but we prayed together every day and asked God to meet us and help us. As the baby got bigger, we dreaded the day when he would be born. What would he look like? I was scared out of my mind.

On October 7, 2001, our little baby boy was born. Bob gave him his name, Robert. His second name, Theodore, is uniquely his and means "divine gift," and that's exactly what he has been to our family. Our other three children have adored him every single day of his life. He is celebrated and loved. His life exudes tons of personality, lots of laughing, and excessive talking! I'm sure the enemy figured this pregnancy would destroy our lives, and at the beginning we barely survived the news. Even through the pain, we tried to keep God's perspective. This baby is the innocent one. He didn't ask for this. But in retrospect we can see the redemption of God. He demonstrated first-hand His ability to take an impossible situation and turn it around into a story of His grace. But it didn't always feel like this.

Put Your Future in God's Hands

When I meet women who have had abortions, I hold them and cry with them. I understand the intensity of such a decision, one that often has nothing to do with whether or not you "believe" in abortion, but rather the desperation and fear of facing your future with this baby. I also have seen the power of God's forgiveness, mercy, and redemption even when an abortion does take place. There is no sin too great that God won't lovingly forgive and restore our future.

When I first found out I was pregnant, I was home alone in my kitchen. I picked up the phone and called an abortion clinic. After giving them the details of the dates, they informed me that because of the very early detection, they could simply send me ten blue pills in the mail – anonymously. Following the simple instructions of one pill per week, my "problem" would be over.

I cried when I hung up the phone and I fell to my knees and sobbed. Our carnal mind will do everything possible to protect our ego and reputation. I didn't want to kill this baby, but desperation drove me to consider the unthinkable.

After resisting the temptation to abort my baby, I begged God for a miscarriage. I get tears as I write this for I love our son with all of my heart. I can't imagine life without him. God knew this, and I thank Him for sparing me from controlling my own future. I wonder how many times I beg God to evacuate me out of my current circumstances and then wonder why He isn't answering my prayers. It's because He wants something much higher – He wants to walk with me through my circumstances and in His loving wisdom develop my character through sustained faith and hope for something I cannot see right now.

God wants to walk with you through your circumstances and in His loving wisdom develop your character through sustained faith and hope for something you cannot see right now.

We are all glad that Robert is alive. If you ever want to read Bob's side of the story and more details about the healing that took place, our book *Marriage Under Cover* is available in bookstores or our Web site, www.bobandaudrey.com. This book has helped tens of thousands of people receive perspective and understanding during affairs. It has also been an aid to pastors and leaders as they walk with couples and bring counsel during these extremely sensitive times.

Most of you may not relate to what I have done directly, but every one of us has felt that we have made wrong choices that have brought irreversible consequences to our lives. As a result we hold onto regret, we wear shame like a cloak, and we re-think what we would do if we could only get a second chance. The time machine hasn't been invented, so there are no do-overs. But what we can do is: Face our issues head on; deal with them in a healthy manner; and trust that God is able to work everything out so we can live our best life for all persons involved.[11]

Remember to grab your journal and take a few minutes to go through the About You section on the next page.

about you

- Have you put expectations on people to be your source of joy and happiness? If so, who? Write out your intention to make God your primary source and others only as contributors.

- Have you made wrong choices that brought irreversible consequences? Write down all the good that can come from this situation.

meditation

Meditate on the hope that God promises, and *imagine* and *feel* what these verses describe as you apply them to your life:

> And we know that God causes everything to work together for the good of those who love God and are called according to his purpose for them. And I am convinced that nothing can ever separate us from God's love. Neither death nor life, neither angels nor demons, neither our fears for today nor our worries about tomorrow—not even the powers of hell can separate us from God's love. No power in the sky above or in the earth below—indeed, nothing in all creation will ever be able to separate us from the love of God that is revealed in Christ Jesus our Lord.[12]

how restoration begins

*We've all made mistakes and carry secrets. Can you
dream of a life of radical transparency where you
have nothing to hide? Discerning who to trust,
refusing to fight back, getting the help you need, and
listening to the right voices will lead to restoration.*

YOU'VE MADE A MISTAKE. You have violated your own
moral code. Maybe nobody knows. Maybe everyone knows. So
what should you do? This chapter is all about what you can do
after the truth has come out to begin the restoration process.

Discern Who You Can Trust and Tell

It is so important to know that this is not the time to isolate
yourself in hopes that over time you will get better. The secrets
you have been keeping have been wearing you out. If you are
in the middle of a current crisis, you need immediate help so

that you don't do any further damage to your situation. I was so surprised that after I confessed to Bob, he immediately called someone for help – the very lifeline we needed in the immediacy of the moment.

You desire intimacy with God, and possibly your husband, and what paves the way to intimacy is purity, and purity starts with honesty and transparency. More than likely the people you contact initially will be your inspiration, but they may not necessarily be the ones who will journey with you through the long haul. There will be several avenues you can take, but you're not going to share with everyone.

You may be in a place where you have a choice as to who you will tell. Whoever you tell or finds out will have an opinion for you. Some will agree with what God's heart is for you, and some will make you feel even worse or give you bad advice. When choosing someone to listen to, you can make no presumptions. Best friends can suddenly turn judgmental, spiritual leaders can give ungodly advice, and professional counselors can stir up unnecessary blame on others. Parents and family members can sometimes step in and want to control. I'm not saying this happens all the time, but I've witnessed all of these on numerous occasions. On the other hand, these could be the best people in the world to choose to trust.

Let's talk about the best people to talk to. Here's a suggested checklist:

- I have more hope after talking to this person
- I feel understood

- This person isn't allowing me to blame others or circumstances
- This person is challenging me to embrace truth
- I feel loved by God after talking to this person

During the first months after finding out about the affair, there were impressionable moments where Bob could not contain his devastation. During these times his eyes would be full of hatred and rage against me. His interrogation and demands for explanation felt like torture. I would cower in his presence and what worth remained was drained from me with every accusing statement. I knew that Bob was going through his own extreme pain and torment that I couldn't fully understand. However, I didn't feel I could express the pain and torment I was going through during this horrific crisis.

During those first painful months, God became more like a father to me than ever before. I clearly remember joining my dad on an errand to Home Depot. I was so relieved to be alone with him where I could be safe, let my guard down, and release the deep-rooted emotions of pain and fear. My dad was full of love and compassion… and even hope and excitement for his new grandchild. But I couldn't get past the pain.

That's what you did, but that's not who you are.

We arrived at the parking lot, and when it was time to go in I simply said, "Dad, go ahead without me. I'm an emotional mess. I'm going to wait in the car." He said, "I'm not going anywhere, Audrey. That's what you *did*, but that's not who you *are*." Those words have never left me. They were spoken from my dad, but were directly from my heavenly Father. I remembered those words, and I held on to that hope for dear life as I lived through the next months of pregnancy. I chose to listen to these words instead of others that came against me.

You too will need to choose carefully who to listen to. It may be a friend, a relative, a spiritual leader, or a counselor. The people who are best for you won't want to leave you where you are. They will want you to make steps toward forgiveness, thankfulness, and wise choices for the future. They will help you to avoid taking the easy way out as a quick fix that won't bring wholeness and true happiness in the end.

The people who are best for you won't want to leave you where you are. They will want you to make steps toward forgiveness, thankfulness, and wise choices for the future.

When it comes to anything in your life that could be labeled scandalous, tell as few people as possible. Have you noticed that people love to spread around juicy information? After I told Bob about the affair, our pastor asked us to keep it completely confidential except for my parents. I'm so thankful for this sound advice that kept us from involving more people that could have gotten hurt. His basic words were, "Situations like this are on a need-to-know-basis." Ask yourself who absolutely needs to know, and then take the next step.

You may be carrying a secret that you haven't told to anyone. Secrets carry a lot of power to condemn you in your own thoughts. There's a temptation to believe a variety of lies: *If people knew they wouldn't love me. I will be rejected. I am forced to keep this a secret to protect others. I would cause too much pain if I confessed. It's better if I just live with this lonely pain, nobody would understand.*

Sharing a secret to a person who is safe is a very healthy thing to do. Recently we spoke at a church in New Orleans, and after hearing our marriage story, several women were able to confess secrets they were harboring in their hearts. We cried and wept together as I was able to share God's perspective of unconditional love, acceptance, and forgiveness. Many times people ask me for specific direction: Do I need to tell my husband? Do I have to tell anyone else?

The worst part about carrying a secret is the guilt and shame you carry around like baggage. You feel like a hypocrite with everyone you know and your self-talk becomes highly negative. It's also easy just to stuff the secret and justify your actions or blame others. As a side note, when it comes to situations that involve abuse, know that the abuse is never your fault and you don't deserve that kind of behavior. But if you will refuse to blame others, you'll be able to focus on yourself so that you can begin to seek the healing your heart needs.

Even though I told Bob, my parents, and our pastor, I did not tell my children or close friends about the pregnancy. I felt like I was putting on an act trying to appear normal and fine. But now when I look back, remaining quiet was the grace of God. He gave me the strength to carry the secret, thus filtering the millions of opinions that would have become instantly and readily available!

When it comes to people asking me for advice, each case is individual in its circumstances and there are no pat answers. Know that, the best counselor, teacher, advisor, and comforter is the Holy Spirit. I guarantee that as you ask God for direction, He will answer the cries of your heart. Intentionally quieting the noise of your mind and emotions and listening to the still small voice in your heart opens the door for you to hear God and follow His direction. God is completely trustworthy. Instead of asking the question, "How can the Word of God apply to my situation?" the question should rather be, "How can I align my life to the Word of God?"

Refuse to Fight Back

Getting into an emotional fight with someone usually ends in regret. When you are being attacked, it's very natural to become defensive and fight back. You say and do things you can't take back. Bob had no idea the amount of pain he was causing me, just as I had little idea of the amount of pain I had caused him. We couldn't understand each other at this point of the crisis. But I refused to lash back, and most importantly, on the inside, I just kept saying to myself, "I forgive him. I caused this pain and he doesn't know what he's doing to me. God does not define me by my selfish sin and mistake. God loves me unconditionally."

As I look back at the initial onset of our crisis, I had no understanding of the amount of pain I caused Bob. It took years of asking God to show me my heart to have the courage to really understand the depth of betrayal I acted out. Even now, ten years later, I will look at Bob, see how he loves me, and know that I don't really understand. I have a lot better of an idea after helping many other couples, but I will never know the extent of pain that resulted from my foolish actions. Even though I have forgiven myself, I will always be sorry for what I did. And I will always be grateful to Bob for forgiving me.

As I speak to women about refusing to fight back, I reassure them that this doesn't make them a doormat, and it doesn't mean that they shouldn't confront the situation once emotions aren't skyrocketing. What it means is that you are a peacemaker and you understand that fighting in the heat of the moment will only punish and hurt each other further. It only takes one to stop a fight! Refusing to fight back diffuses the negative energy eventually! The only way to live like this is to embrace humility and lay down the right to hurt the one who is hurting you. This is not easy by any means – but so worth it in the end!

It's impossible to lay down your rights without ridding your heart of pride. Pride is an ugly sin that makes thriving relationships virtually impossible. Even though you give up your pride, you never have to give up your dignity. You are a beautiful daughter of the King. You are royalty, and even though you serve one another in love, being a peacemaker means you refuse to fight back, but your dignity stays intact.

Ask for Help

Suppressed pain would have killed me. It would have shown up in sickness or driven me insane – who knows. I just know that I had to express the pain to someone. I didn't want anyone to know how bad it was. I didn't want my mom to worry about me. I did most of my "talking" in my journal where I was honest and transparent. I addressed my letters to God knowing that He loved me and wanted to help me. The Lord provided a few trusted friends and counselors who helped me sort through my scattered and often confused emotions.

A rather spontaneous opportunity came up for me to talk to Dr. Don Colbert. (See www.drcolbert.com. His book related to this subject is *Toxic Emotions – Understand the Mind-Body-Spirit Connection that can Heal or Destroy You*). He and his wife were visiting my parents' home for dinner after visiting our city to be guests on our daily TV show. It took courage, but I asked them to help me. It had been two years since Robert was born. Bob and I were doing OK. We were committed to our marriage and stable in our relationship.

Dr. Don and his wife Mary recognized what they called "acute grief" within my heart. This was a surprise to me. I would never have guessed this one! I am naturally a happy, spontaneous personality, able to cover up what was really going on in my heart. I covered this grief even to myself. They proceeded to tell me that acute grief is much more than overlaying sadness. Acute grief gets trapped inside a person as the result of a death-blow, a sudden loss, or a horrific crisis. I was more than happy to pray about this and deal with it in any way they suggested!

Be Willing to Visit Painful Places

How do you get rid of grief? Dr. Don and Mary were willing to journey with me in the place of prayer. But before we proceeded, they said they needed to "check" my belief system. They began to ask me key questions:

- Would it be a good thing for me to forgive myself? *Yes*.
- Would it be good for Bob for me to forgive me? *Yes*.
- Was it necessary? *Yes*.
- Was it the right thing to do? *Yes*.
- Do I deserve to forgive myself?

When they came to that last question *Do I deserve to forgive myself?* there was dead silence. The answer was no. Definitely not. I had forgiven Bob for the times he had rejected me and interrogated me. I had forgiven the people who accused me, judged me, labeled me, and talked behind my back. However, if I could separate myself from the Audrey who did that and place her in front of me, this is what I would say: "Audrey, you caused me more pain than I was ever meant to bear. Audrey, your selfish choice made me hurt my loving husband, my precious kids, and my dear parents. Audrey, you destroyed my entire life and now I'll never ever be as happy as I was before. I will never have the freedom to laugh again because of you and your selfish pleasure. Audrey, you embarrassed me and ruined my reputation forever. Audrey, in one month of stupidity you destroyed my entire life. Audrey, I reject you and I hate you."

It was all of these feelings I had never recognized before that kept me living in shame. Grief signifies loss, and the fact that I was diagnosed with acute grief meant I lost much more than I thought when I gave myself to another man. Deep inside I was grieving and didn't even know it.

Be Willing to See Yourself Differently

The doctor asked me to remember this pain and all most painful circumstances surrounding this crisis. He asked me to let go and release the grief. I did. I cried and cried. OK, I wailed. Thinking of how if felt to tell my kids. Remembering how sad I was every night when I put my face on the pillow, alone with my thoughts.

I then imagined the *other* Audrey and the ugly sin that caused astronomical pain. Instead of judging her and condemning her behavior, I understood God's love for her even in the middle of a disgusting pile of sin. In the same way He accepted and loved her back, I needed to do the same and embrace the part of me that made the deadly choices and caused the crisis.

After at least 20 minutes of emotional intensity, basically unloading years of locked-in grief, the crying subsided. I remember the peace that encompassed me. The room was silent. It was a tender moment in God's presence. My eyes were closed. It felt like I was an open, thirsty vessel and my heavenly Father began filling every fiber of my being with value, worth, and extravagant love. Then a picture appeared in my mind of myself clothed in the most beautiful, pure, white and glistening robe of righteousness. I looked so content and so loved. God spoke to my heart in that moment and said, "Will you agree to see yourself the way I see you?" I took a deep breath, smiled gently and said, "Yes."

That's when everything changed. It was as if the "cloak of shame" I had been wearing since the affair fell off instantly. It was like fragrant oil of joy came down from heaven drenching my beautiful robe making it slippery. I knew why this was so important. You see, up until that point, I lived life walking into malls, my place of work, and church and people recognized me. The rumor mill was alive with the news of my un- forgivable scandalous behavior. I could

Everything changed the moment I agreed to see myself the way God sees me.

feel people judging me. It was as if they had black permanent markers writing big Xs on me. The words were not audible, but their power would overshadow me: *There's the girl who did THAT. She calls herself a Jesus girl! She doesn't deserve anything good to happen to her. She deserves to be punished and disquali- fied for what she did.* But now…oh, now things were so differ- ent because my beautiful and pure robe was slippery. Those Xs couldn't stick. I was free!

Jesus took every bit of punishment that I deserved on the cross. He paid the price and bore the penalty. And because of His indescribable expression of love for me, I could be free to love, be loved, and forgive myself in order to be in agreement with Him. It's taken me all of my forty-five years of life to begin to fathom what Jesus really did for me on that cross when He died for me. I'm pretty sure my entire future including eternity will be spent receiving and revealing the richness and depth of the love He has for me, and adoring and worshipping Him in response.

Since that night, February 13, 2004, I have never been the same. I received the indescribable gift of Jesus' righteousness. It was never mine anyway! The Bible clearly tells us that we will never be able to be perfect. In fact, the Bibles says that the best we have to offer is like filthy rags to God.[13] Religion will try and tell us that we have to follow rules in order to earn our way to heaven, or God will be disappointed in us and punish us. God saw me, and in His love He forgave me and loved me. I'm a daughter of the King, an adopted heir. All of this is because of the death, burial, and resurrection of Jesus Christ.

Edit Your Thoughts and Outside Voices

To say that was a life-changing night is an understatement. Instead of doubting, thinking this bliss wouldn't last, I made a choice to be ready when thoughts came to my head. We usually receive messages in a series as one thought leads to another, either opening up to God's voice or lies of the enemy. This meant that I had to be intentional the next time judgments and accusations came firing at me. I was ready!

I kept the mental picture I had of me in the robe of righteousness in the forefront of my mind. When I sensed that someone was judging me or was tempted to condemn myself, I stopped the cycle and remembered the truth of who I was because of Jesus. This process of persuading my heart of the truth lasted for a few years, but I can say that today I am fully persuaded. Nobody has the power to take that truth from my heart. I am clean, I am forgiven, and I am established in God's love for me. Someone may attempt to challenge my point of view, but it's permanently stamped on my heart. I am loved, cherished, and forgiven.

In the next chapter we'll look at practical steps that you can take to forgive yourself and begin to love yourself back to life.

about you

- Are you carrying a secret? What don't you share with anyone?

- Who in your life you can trust with your secrets?

- Describe your version of the perfect father.

- Now thank God in heaven that He has every attribute of a perfect father.

meditation

From the book Song of Songs, these verses describe God's amazing love. The *seal* from Jesus today is the Holy Spirit, placed with in us, assuring us that what God will promise He will perform. As you meditate on these verses, ask God to intensify your understanding of His love.

> Place me like a seal over your heart, like a seal on your arm. For love is as strong as death, its jealousy as enduring as the grave. Love flashes like fire, the brightest kind of flame. Many waters cannot quench love, nor can rivers drown it. If a man tried to buy love with all his wealth, his offer would be utterly scorned.[14]

chapter 5

7 steps to forgive yourself

Forgiving yourself is no easy task. It requires an
intentional and ongoing decision to choose life,
embrace humility, and put justice in God's hands.
Learning to be your own best friend leads to
an ethical, authentic life.

YOU ARE NOT ALONE. I meet many people who are
longing for unconditional self-love and freedom from self-
incrimination. "I wish I could forgive myself," people tell me,
or, "I'm afraid I'll never be able to forgive myself." After hearing
my story, many women ask me, "How do you forgive yourself?"
They're not asking if it's possible or the right thing to do, they
just want to know *how* to do it because they're in pain.

I believe that living a life of forgiveness is the most en-
ergy-efficient and productive way to live. I believe that self-

forgiveness is essentially inseparable from self-respect and self-responsibility. Forgiving yourself and loving yourself doesn't mean you can excuse yourself from hard work, self-sacrifice, and life's responsibilities. The self-forgiving person is *not* (as many believe, or at least fear) a selfish person. It is the person who remains stuck in self-doubt and self-condemnation who will lead the more self-centered, less-productive life. They will put greater expectations on others to meet their needs with less capacity to love others unconditionally.

Forgiving yourself is actually embracing full responsibility for the life and gifts God has graciously given you. Forgiveness is agreeing with God about how He sees you. This is a daily exercise, not just something to do when your conscience is bugging you or you start to see negative consequences. So let's look at how to forgive yourself (and others in some cases) and begin loving yourself to life.

1. Choose Life

Forgiving yourself usually doesn't happen by accident. It requires an intentional, proactive decision to move forward and change the way you think about yourself. Why not declare this right now: *I want to live. I want to really live. Today I begin the process of forgiving myself and learning how to see myself the way God sees me — wanted, loved, and accepted.* An intention is not just a wish or a good idea. An intention is when you make a goal and couple it with strong desire for change. You begin imagining yourself free and even feeling the emotions of what it will feel like. You are experiencing the end from the beginning. That is faith. Your statement of faith is: "I *am* free from shame. I *am* completely forgiven. Therefore, I forgive myself."

I strongly suggest that you record the journey of forgiving yourself in a personal journal. Write out your thoughts and feelings through each step, and also God's response to you. Because of the magnitude of this exercise and the potential it has to change your life, it is best done in a quiet place where you can be as private as possible. I imagine a place where I commune with God in my heart and call it my secret place.

2. Bring it to Light

The enemy of your soul thrives in darkness. Bringing the reality of your heart condition to light will quickly begin your journey to forgiving yourself. You are experiencing negative emotions, whether they are shame, fear, anger, or self-pity. Ask God where the root of these emotions has come from. Was there an incident? Do you have an abiding feeling of worthlessness? Review exactly what is taking place in your heart and examine why you feel disappointed or angry with yourself. Ask yourself these and other related questions:

- Did I fail to live up to my own expectations or someone else's?
- Where did those expectations come from?
- Am I embarrassed or humiliated?
- Who observed the behavior, and am I afraid of what they will think?
- What prevailing thoughts and emotions are attached to the memory?

Bringing light will give opportunity for greater understanding as you move through the process of forgiving and loving yourself to life. I can't emphasize enough how much courage it takes to face the dark places of your life. I am so proud of you for taking this step and can reassure you that freedom and peace are your reward!

3. Talk to a Compassionate Listener

Tell your story and sort through your own feelings with a trusted friend. If you are not yet able to share with anyone, write down your thoughts in a journal and read them out loud to God. Either way, be honest about what you did or failed to do and how you feel about yourself. Observing another person's compassionate response can help you begin to offer yourself that same compassion. You need to be validated as the precious person that you are.

Without placing blame on people or circumstances, recall the surrounding conditions: stress, ignorance, busyness, carelessness, outright sin, or a simple mistake. I am amazed at the new understanding I receive when I can talk out loud and even think out loud with a safe confidante. Fresh understanding and perspective seem to flow out of honest and vulnerable conversation. It's almost as if there are things that are entrapped in our minds, that if anyone really knew what I was thinking or feeling, they wouldn't love me. This keeps us enslaved to the confusion and chaos of our vain imaginations. So bringing them to light again exposes the darkness, removing the ammunition the enemy will use against you.

4. Embrace Humility and Truth

Many people believe that humility is groveling in front of others or thinking we are not good and others are. God gives grace to those who chose humility, but the Bible says that He resists the proud.[15] Those who are humble understand that left to their own resources they are weak, but because of Jesus, they lack nothing. Godly humility is being totally comfortable with who you are in Jesus. Humility is coming into agreement with the person God says you are. The expression of humility is confessing that you need God – that you are not capable of living life on your own, and you don't want to live another day without knowing God as your source for everything.

Confess the areas that you have failed. Without making excuses or blaming others, take full responsibility for the mistakes you have made. Ask God to forgive you for your unbelief, that is, your unwillingness to believe that you are truly forgiven. Receive His forgiveness. Decide that you can learn from this pain and you will come out different.

If there is anything I have learned through the crisis we went through, it's that the truth really does set you free.

Many people shy away from the truth because they are afraid of what it will reveal. I used to be scared of confrontation or admitting my weaknesses, but if there is anything I have learned through the crisis we went through, it's that the truth really does set you free. Instead of avoiding uncomfortable situations, or ignoring my negative emotions in hopes that they'll go away, I attack them! Dr. Jim Richards says, "Coping is not conquering!"

In order to conquer, you set your intention and you become a determined overcomer.

Maybe you had an abortion, destroyed a relationship, or made a bad financial investment. Maybe you drove your kids away, have a secret eating disorder, or another addiction. Maybe you're in the middle of an affair. There are a few important decisions to make. Let God love you and heal your broken heart. Next, gather enough courage to say yes to His plan and be willing to face the reality of your destructive behavior.

5. Turn Justice Over to God

I wanted to punish myself for my mistake. I subconsciously believed that if I inflicted suffering upon myself, I would somehow neutralize the feeling of guilt. This is taking justice into my own hands instead of turning it over to our just God. We often don't forgive ourselves because we don't feel we have been punished enough. So we punish ourselves.

So what is justice? We often think that justice is when a person gets what he or she deserves. Well if any of us were to get what we really deserve, I don't think we would like it! On my own I could never pay enough to cancel out the punishment for what I did. Jesus has stepped in and willingly paid the debt by sacrificing His own life. He paid for my sin so that I don't have to. Because of what Jesus purchased for me and because Jesus lives in me, I don't get what I deserve, I get what He deserves. Because Jesus paid for my sins, I am free from the punishment that I would otherwise have to endure.

Let God make this situation right – that's true justice. God is pursuing you with His unconditional love hoping that you'll receive His righteousness that He paid dearly for. Forgiveness never makes a wrong right. Our fear is that if I forgive yourself, I am then condoning my behavior and I am doomed to repeat it again. Forgiveness is made possible because of the love of God and is a gift to me so that I can in return extend forgiveness to others.

6. Never Give Up

There is nothing you have done that is beyond forgiveness. Forgiveness won't always take away the pain or the consequences of your sin, but it will lead you to a life of everlasting joy and freedom. When the pain of your mistake or weakness returns, or if you fall, get back up. Brush yourself off, get cleaned up and continue to start walking with Him and others again.

Forgiving yourself takes time. During the process, there is much to learn so that you don't wander back and repeat the same cycle. God forgives you instantly, but our journey to wholeness is paved with precious stones of humility, accompanied by an endless source of grace, resulting in a life free from regret and full of joy and peace.

In time you'll find your smile again as you see yourself from God's perspective.

In time you'll find your smile again as you see yourself from His perspective. You'll start loving again and skipping through life with dreams in your heart. Happy endings can come true. No one can live your destiny except you, and no one can take it away unless you let them. So don't give up.

7. Be Your Own Best Friend

The final step in forgiving yourself is learning to stop the self-degrading thoughts of judgment and condemnation. If we were to take an honest inventory of how many negative messages we send ourselves in a day, we would be appalled. The expectations we put on ourselves is ludicrous.

One morning God challenged me to treat myself *exactly* like I treat my best friend. What a concept! I absolutely love my girlfriends and I would consider myself someone who is good at being a true friend. In order to actually treat myself like my best friend, the first thing I had to do was pretend there was *another* one of me across the table. What's the first thing I would say to her? I had to keep thinking…she's my best friend…what would I say to my best friend? First of all, I would celebrate her, appreciate her, notice the things she is doing well, and remind her that she's valued beyond belief. If she was going through a tough time, we would talk it out and possibly pray together asking for God's perspective. I always want my friends to see themselves the way God sees them – absolutely beautiful, a precious and priceless treasure, and a daughter of the King.

I started doing this and my thought life began to change. I was more patient as a wife, less needy as a friend, and less demanding as a mother. When I'm my own best friend, it protects me from false accusation. I would never say mean things to my friends, so I stop saying mean things to myself! Interestingly enough, it also protects me from self-pity. In the past when I felt unappreciated, I would think about the fact that nobody sees all the work I'm doing. Now I just start telling myself the truth, "Audrey, you are being responsible today. Great job! And by the way, I appreciate your attitude too!"

Another thing I'm doing more is resting. Even if it's a five-minute break, I'll take the luxury of closing my eyes and imagine God leading me to green pastures…and crystal-clear-blue waters. Many of us work extremely hard and don't get the encouragement we need. Instead of expecting encouragement from people, you can begin to receive astronomical amounts of love from yourself through appreciating the things you do *and* the way God made you. We have the choice and the responsibility to decide what our self-talk will be. Let's agree with God's love for us. We can do this!

Where Do You Start?

Let's start in the morning. You wake up. Pay very close attention to your thoughts. My bathroom is loaded with mirrors – full length ones that capture every angle. Lovely! I actually do not work out every day as the magazines tell me I should, especially a woman my age who is losing muscle mass by the minute. The result? I think my son, Robert, said it best when I was waving good-bye to him the other day. He exclaimed, "Mom, you can wave your arm in two places at one time!"

Do we really want to venture lower than my arms? I could confess all the things hanging on my body. My arms are nothing compared to my saggy butt that waves in a special way every time I walk. Let's just conclude this section saying I'm very thankful for clothes. Naked me wouldn't be my best presentation to the world.

I really don't mind laughing at myself. The truth is that Bob loves every inch of me and I am thankful for the body God gave me. Could I devote more time and effort to firming up a little? Definitely. Part of loving myself is taking care of my body. But the point is that I would never, ever, EVER talk to *you* like that. So why would *I* start my day by speaking to myself like that? Would I meet you for coffee, give you the once-over with a detective-magnifying glass, and point out your every imperfection and gladly use words to describe what they are? Never. Yet, we are so quick to speak this way of ourselves.

Let's talk about you. I know that given the chance you and I would have an amazing time together. If we were out for coffee, we would get to know each other. We would laugh, talk, open our hearts, possibly cry, and definitely hug each other. I would hope to encourage you exactly where you need it for that moment, cherishing the richness of meeting you. After all, we are sisters in God's family! We are definitely going to dance together in heaven one day.

Another layer of self-forgiveness came when I realized I could be as nice and loving to myself as I am to my best friends.

Maybe this concept is over the top, but for me another layer of self-forgiveness came when I realized I could be as nice and loving to myself as I am to my best friends. This concept goes much deeper than outer appearance. Maybe you have been mean to yourself for years. Maybe you have focused on your failures, downfalls, and regrets each day while sporting a smile. You are truly ready to become your own best friend. As the day continues and you leave the bathroom, you will continue to be nice to yourself as you encounter people, situations, and challenges. Be determined not only to love yourself back to life, but also come to the point where you actually enjoy your own company.

about you

Finding peace in your heart means coming to terms with mistakes that you've made. This forgiveness exercise can be extremely painful and takes a tremendous amount of courage. It is not designed to bring you shame, but rather affirm you with value and unconditional love. I promise you that the reward is worth it. Follow this general outline:

thankfulness

Begin to thank God for His truth, His perspective, and His opinion. Write down your words of appreciation to Him and persuade your heart that you never have to question Him. Some suggestions of thankfulness are:

- Thank you God that you do not hold my mistakes against me.

- Thank you God that you don't identify me by my failures.

- Thank you God that you have forgiven me completely.

- Thank you God for loving me unconditionally.

repentance

Write down the regrets and mistakes that you have stuffed down to the deep places of your heart – the ones you try not to think about. Remember that this is private and intimate between you and God. You can be blatantly honest. Start your sentences: "Thank you God that you have forgiven me for…" You may feel drawn to pour your heart out to God. Don't hold back.

blessing

- Ask God how He feels about you. Write down what you hear. God's voice will always bring extravagant love, light, hope, redemption, and freedom.

- Ask Him what He loves most about you. Even though he's proud of you for all you do, allow Him to express His love to you for who you are.

- Ask God to help you imagine the bright future He has for you. Dream about what it feels like to experience your best days ahead of you. Your past doesn't dictate your future!

chapter 6

from full of me
to full of god

*God doesn't love you because you're beautiful. You
are beautiful because God loves you. Liking yourself
does not mean you are self-absorbed, it means you've
discovered the secrets to loving life, making you an
expert at loving others.*

AFTER FIVE CHAPTERS of "like yourself, love your life,"
my prayer is that you are discovering new levels of peace in
your mind and joy in your heart. During the forgiveness exercise, you have emptied yourself of the old you. God is making
things new in your life. You are establishing a new normal!

The fears, guilt, anger, resentment, and shame are now in
the past and there they will stay. It is vital that you immediately
fill yourself with everything good that comes from God.

How to be Full of God

The other day I was reading the Bible and came across two scriptures that jumped out at me.

> God…who *fills* all things everywhere with Himself… and we are *filled* with the richest measure of His divine presence.[16]

We are full of God! Full of His "divine presence"! And when this is the desire of our heart, there is absolutely no room to be full of ourselves! This explains how we can love ourselves completely while living for others, and cause everyone we encounter to feel loved, valued, and extremely important.

I fill myself up with God by intentionally thinking about Him and including Him in my day-to-day activities. I place great importance on stopping my activities to mediate on scripture verses. I listen to music and sing along, and I read books and listen to messages by people that speak God's truth. You will be unique in how you spend time with Him, and He will give you creative ideas of how to keep yourself full of Him!

Not An Option

Knowing God as my Source and filling myself up with Him is not an option. Bob and I often get asked the question, "How do you tell your story over and over again? Is it even healthy to remember that pain and re-live the trauma?" The truth is that I never feel drained or shamed after revealing the details of how God rescued our marriage. In fact, if anything, it feels like worship to God as we tell the stories of how He led us to the right place at the right time. He walked with us and cried with us through our sorrow and grief. And the best part is that we now have the opportunity to communicate extravagant hope, for if God can do this for us, He can do it for anyone.

The reason we can tell our story over and over is because it's really *Him* who is living His life through us. The Bible says, "It is no longer I who live, but Christ lives in me."[17] At the end of our story people don't look at us and think, "Wow, look at what *they* have done." Rather they realize that in the midst of our mistakes and grief, God met us, and look what *He* can do! The glory they see is the outward manifestation of the inward dwelling presence of God. We are full of Him!

I recently saw a TV show for teenagers. A group of young adults were putting on a play as part of an acting contest and were improvising as they went along. Two boys were competing for one girl's affection. With wisdom and insight she quickly saw through the rich boy who was highly attracted to her physical beauty. When she confronted the poor boy with honorable intentions she asked him, "Do you love me just because I'm beautiful?" He paused, looked deep in her eyes and answered, "No, you're beautiful because I love you...."

Your opinion of what you physically look like in this moment is not important. You are beautiful because God loves you!

I'd like to say the same thing to you: *You are beautiful because God loves you.* Your opinion of what you physically look like in this moment is not important. You might believe you aren't beautiful at all; in fact, people may have even told you that with hurtful words and damaging comments. But that has no precedence in understanding your true beauty. Instead of being mad at God for creating you with flaws, why not consider how He sees you. Instead of hating yourself for your mistakes and failures, why not see yourself clothed in a beautiful, white, glistening robe of unconditional love and forgiveness? Why not dare to believe that when He looks at you He smiles with adoration and says, "Ah…my beautiful one…."

about you

Before we consider some of the dangers of being full of ourselves, let's explore the wonder of being full of God. Write down some practical ways that you can fill yourself with God's presence.

meditation

On the next page is a personal entry from my journal. I have found that recording intimate conversations between God and myself brings solidity to our relationship.

Lover-God says:

To my precious princess.

Every once in awhile you forget. You start thinking, "Oh, I'm just one in millions. You feel this way about everybody. I'm just one person."

Pause…and listen…

"You are the one I love and adore."

My Response:

I hear Your words and I respond with adoration and want to give myself to You. I feel so safe with You. So fulfilled. So protected by You. I feel cherished.

You are my song. I carry the fragrance of Your pursuit. I love You more than words could say. I feel the warmth of Your hand in mine. I don't have to try. I just want You. All of You. I will be Yours – I will be Your beautiful one.

Now take a few moments to write out your own conversation between yourself and God.

Beware of Self-Love Counterfeits

Getting free from unhealthy self-love isn't just a good idea to make you socially acceptable. Self-absorbed people are potentially dangerous in that they can say things and do things that damage other's self-worth. Because they are mostly thinking about themselves, they unknowingly are insensitive to the feelings of those around them, and disregard the lethal messages they are sending.

Being full of God means there's no room for self-centeredness. You have a choice. You can love and accept yourself, which is healthy if it is based on agreement with God and how He values your life. Or you can be consumed and absorbed with yourself in attempts to feed your ego and achieve approval and acceptance apart from God. None of us want to be self-absorbed or conceited, so simply be aware of the counterfeits of self-love, pursue humility, and ask God to purify your heart of selfish motives.

My passion and hope is that through my own story of forgiving myself you will be inspired to do the same. I realize that some might say, "Hold your horses, Audrey! If I love and accept myself as I am, does it mean I negate accountability and personal responsibility? If I'm not hard on myself, does that mean I let myself take a vacation from my life and just follow my every whim that promises rest and pleasure? Do I actually get to escape? If I accept my failures, does that mean I allow myself to continue in wrong behavior?"

A common assumption is that self-forgiveness is a snazzy, politically correct, socially-acceptable way to let yourself off the hook by avoiding accountability and personal responsibility. This is absolutely not true. In fact, a more powerful and accurate definition of forgiveness is quite the opposite: self-forgiveness is the natural starting place for anyone who wants to lead an ethical life as free from hypocrisy as is humanly possible.

Self-forgiveness is the natural starting place for anyone who wants to lead an ethical life as free from hypocrisy as is humanly possible.

It's important to know the counterfeits of self-love. The last thing I want to do is love myself and get obnoxious about it. You've met someone like this. This behavior can be repulsive. One characteristic that all self-absorbed people share is that they are completely oblivious to their obnoxious behavior and are confused when others don't give them the attention and notoriety they obviously deserve! There are different expressions of counterfeit self-lovers, but maybe you'll recognize some of these:

The Player. He's arrogant, over-confident, disrespectful, self-centered, and revels in the fact that he intrigues everyone. You are amazed that some people actually get sucked in by his ability to flatter and sweet talk his way into the very thing he wants. This guy knows how to butter up, smooth talk, and is obviously crazy about his own hotness.

Ms. Know-It-All. This woman knows it ALL. She has the ability to fix everyone and gives herself free reign to correct anyone who doesn't line up with her system of values. She's a control freak on steroids and has no idea that what she's doing is repulsive. In fact, she prides herself in helping everyone around her. By the way, she's always right, completely perfect, and has all the answers.

Mr. Important. He's God's gift to the world. He promotes himself, talks about himself, and dramatizes his own significance to the point that he believes his own lies in order to magnify his worth. He's not interested in others, doesn't recognize others' significance or achievements, but places high priority on making sure that people in high position notice him in order to elevate his status.

Miss Popular. She probably doesn't realize that every conversation is centered around her. If someone prettier, funnier, or smarter shows up, she quickly protects her rank by backbiting and gossip (while still maintaining her proper image). She loves to be the center of attention and loves to hear herself talk, and will revert to interrupting and dominating, convinced that she's everyone's favorite.

Those who are self-absorbed do things primarily to benefit themselves. They put their feelings first, can't do anything when they don't feel good, and are easily swayed by their emotions. In every situation, they are more concerned with themselves than others and prefer personal glory to team victories. A self-absorbed person can often use their looks to get what they want, get angry when they don't get what they want, dramatize their suffering, are wealth seeking, superficial, manipulative, narcissistic, and their ego is never satisfied. They are just plain full of themselves. Whew! I don't know about you, but this is exactly what I don't want to be!

The result of counterfeit self-love, which is narcissism, is that the people around you feel inferior. The narcissist, when taken to the utter core, is wrestling with significance and searching for worth. However, when we truly love ourselves because God loves us, people around us will feel important and our hearts will be at rest, no longer seeking affirmation for survival, but at peace, knowing true love.

What if I find myself participating in self-absorbed behavior? Does that mean I need to shame myself or knock myself in my rightful place by calling myself some bad names? Actually, the exact opposite is true. I need to continue to persuade my heart that I don't need any of those things do derive my worth, confirm my value, or prove my importance. I am already approved and highly significant because of how Jesus feels about me.

It is out of my healthy self-love that I can consider others as more important than myself. I can approach situations and others with a heart of humility, die to self and find resurrected life in Jesus. The narcissist is willing to hurt and use others, but we love ourselves so much that we value others and recognize the value that God has for them. In a nutshell, those who are self-absorbed value themselves *above* others, and those who truly love themselves value themselves *and* others.

Those who are self-absorbed value them-selves above others, and those who truly loves themselves value themselves and others.

There's nothing wrong with wanting to feel important, popular, beautiful, smart, or right. It's when we need others to feed these attributes in us that we crash out of balance and seek answers where they cannot be found. What does it take in you to feel important? Does the whispered love of your heavenly Father fill that need in your heart?

In my journey to value others, I can be intentional about certain behaviors. I can make a conscious choice to listen intently when someone is speaking to me. I can encourage their accomplishments and never consider another human unimportant or insignificant. I attempt to remember that I don't have to be right, I don't have to have the answer, and I refuse to flatter someone to get what I want.

Giving Yourself Some Attention

One of the best ways to protect yourself from counterfeit self-love is to ensure you are getting the attention you need. My friend's husband owns a pest control business. The other day when I asked how things were going, she mentioned that one of the trucks they use for the business was having transmission problems. We casually talked about the expenses that incur with vehicles. It's never enjoyable to spend money on a transmission!

I started to think about her and the successful business that they run. Few people stop to realize the overhead and expenses just in having service trucks. Her husband is smart to keep those trucks in great shape. Is he being selfish for taking excellent care of these vehicles? Is he being selfish to make sure that each truck has sufficient gasoline, the oil is changed on schedule, and the tires are filled with the recommended air pressure? Absolutely not, his priority to care for those trucks is not about being selfish. It's about being smart. Without regular, quality maintenance the trucks would eventually require much more time and attention, not to mention money.

People are the same way. The better we take care of ourselves, the more effective we will be as wives, mothers, friends, and daughters. When I have a noisy, neglected engine rattling under my hood, I will be distracted and unfocused on the work at hand. When I "run out of gas," I won't be able to show up (mentally and emotionally) where I'm needed. If I truly love myself and fill myself with God, I will be able to embrace my sphere of influence as a mom, wife, friend, and daughter. I will understand the importance of taking care of myself so that I can give to others. I will understand the reward of being generous. As I have been completely loved, I can easily love others unconditionally.

about you

- How do you make others feel when they are around you? Do they feel valued and important?

- Who or what makes you feel significant and worthwhile? Consider if you are searching for significance and worth apart from God.

- Do you have a need to feel important and be recognized? What ways do you prefer to be recognized and appreciated?

- Do you give yourself enough attention? What are a few healthy ways to give yourself the attention that you need?

- In what areas in your life do you need a "tune up"?

meditation

Cure yourself of the affliction of caring how you appear to others. Concern yourself only with how you appear before God, concern yourself only with the idea that God may have of you. ~ Miguel De Unamuno

transformation of the heart

Your heart is the essence of who you are. Finding peace in your heart is discovering true beauty and pleasure…and the result is joy! Joy is the passionate fuel that generates energy and strength in your life.

Think of the moment you were first born. God had this great idea, and it was you! He examined you and thought to Himself, "When would be the perfect time to put this one on the earth?" You entered life and very quickly embarked on a life-long treasure hunt: the pursuit of happiness. You have a unique personality and your own set of passions—things you love and dreams in your heart—but nevertheless, you have a desire to explore and find the happy ending to each chapter in your life.

Since childhood, we dream and imagine the life that lies before us. As a little girl I remember laying my head on the pillow, closing my eyes and imagining that I was Sleeping Beauty and one day my prince would come and capture my heart. I imagined my future full of sunshine, kisses, and dreams coming true.

As I got older, I learned that there is pain along my path, not everyone liked me, and I sometimes made mistakes. Wouldn't it be great if on the day of your birth you popped out with a treasure map in your hand? How convenient. On the map is a sparkly gold path called "true happiness" and you simply frolic and skip through life having everything you need and enjoying everything you want.

Too bad we don't have that treasure map. Instead, we spend each of our days trying to find that particular path to find happiness. And often we don't fair well. That friend we thought would fill our heart ends up betraying us. The cupcake we thought would make us happy puts us on a sugar-high and we're left with regret when it wears off. Losing that fifty pounds that should have made us happy definitely made us look different, but we still have to fight the battle of knowing that we are loved, accepted, and beautiful regardless of our outward appearance. That truckload of money we thought would make us happy left us empty. That spouse we thought would make us happy feels more like a project. And finding our purpose in life seems like a never-ending battle.

Don't get me wrong – I love cupcakes, I love losing weight, I would love to win a lottery, I love being married, and I love to fulfill purpose! But what do I do when I've eaten the cupcake, I've gained the weight, I've spent all my money, I'm not even married, or I don't even like being married, and I'm too disillusioned to ever consider my reason for living? I've heard these statements too many times from women who don't like themselves or their life.

What would you ask for if you could have absolutely anything? I'm guessing common responses would include lots of money, a perfect relationship, or perfect health. Bob and I have a dear friend and mentor, Dr. James Richards, who helped us understand that people don't really want these things. On a deeper level, we all desire the pleasure that we believe we would receive if we had them.

I am on a quest to find out what God has to say about pleasure. He's the one who created us in minute detail. He knows best what I want underneath the surface. So, what do you *really* want? What's the dream of your heart? Discovering what brings you true pleasure will answer those questions. Interestingly enough, finding true pleasure and joy has nothing to do with changing your outside circumstances, but rather changing your heart.

Finding true pleasure and joy has nothing to do with changing your outside circumstances, but rather changing your heart.

A Healthy Heart is Like a Healthy Garden

Your heart is the essence of who you are. The place to start to find pleasure is discovering peace in your heart. That peace results in joy. And joy is passionate fuel that generates energy and strength in your life. Joy is the contagious flow of life that gives a spring to your step and pushes you to rise above the circumstances. So the question is, how do you find peace in your heart?

I find it easier to talk about "heart things" using a word-picture. We're obviously not talking about your physical heart, but rather the deepest part of you – the place where your will and emotions meet your decisions and your passion.

Think of your heart as a garden. There are flowers, scents, trees, walkways and paths, and sections to your garden. Even though you can't see your garden with your physical eyes, you actually live out of this place, which is your heart. Your thoughts, your words, your reactions, and your responses all start here. The health of your heart determines how much joy, peace, and contentment you have in this life.

Several years ago, I realized that I didn't like some of the fruit that was growing on the trees in my garden. The fragrances being produced in my life weren't all daisies and roses, if you know what I mean. My heart-garden was all right in some areas, but there were many places I wouldn't dare visit because of the weeds, thorns, and pests. It looked like forest fires had left some places black, charred, and stripped of life. The stench of rotten fruit was distasteful

This is how my garden-condition affected me. I was full of fear. I hated the thought of failure and was apprehensive of my future. I worried about money and I obsessed about my weight. I felt insecure and thought I had to try harder to fulfill my purpose. I wasn't living up to my own expectations. I easily felt guilty for my shortcomings and had come to the realization that I was a disappointment in many areas of my life. When people didn't choose me or rejected me, I would spend days wondering why. I evaluated my weaknesses constantly and introspection easily became self-destructive.

God loves making things new. I leap on the inside when I think of the verse in the Bible where God says,

> "And I will give you a new heart, and I will put a new spirit in you. I will take out your stony, stubborn heart and give you a tender, responsive heart."[18]

He wants to be my gardener and rip out the weeds, thorns, and overgrown mess. He wants to lovingly plant seeds, water and nurture these seeds, and witness new growth in me that produces strong vitality, security, and value. He wants to smile with me as the exotic flowers, blooming bushes, and strong fruit-bearing trees envelop the sparse spaces – producing irresistible aromas, earth-shaking beauty, and satisfying fruit. That's the kind of garden that I want to spend time in.

That's the dream, but where and how do we start in the process of re-inventing the garden of our heart? If you're a woman, I can probably guess that you're as tired as I have been. Tired of doing the same things, tired of being under-appreciated, and tired of responsibilities that take a toll on our bodies, minds, and emotions. Because of weariness, you are probably grieving. God created you to be a girl who dances with Him, has intimate moments, is free to belly-laugh, and is quick to forgive.

And it when it comes to change in your life, your first reaction might be to deal with the obvious: Get your husband to simply give you the love and appreciation you deserve, get your kids to smarten up, and find a way to have more money. As long as you're still blaming any of those things, you're not ready for true change in your heart. My sister-in-law Lisa recently said, "As long as your reward is tied to another human being, you will never understand what real joy is in Jesus." We are going to seek *true* pleasure, and that can only be found in your heart as you make the changes in yourself. You won't get a brand new husband, kids, or bank account (although those things may improve), but you will get pleasure, freedom, and rest, and you don't have to wait for anything on the outside to change. It starts now, and it starts with you.

No Matter Where You Go, There You Are

I recently talked to a woman married twenty-three years to her husband; she's been unhappy since the second month of their marriage. She heard our marriage story and found me to ask for help. She looked longingly into my eyes, almost begging for me to give her an answer. She wore grief and despair like an obvious piece of clothing. Not only did she lose the dream in her heart for a happy marriage, but felt like she had lost twenty-three years of her life, where she didn't feel like she could be herself.

She used to be creative, artistic, and successful. She believes her husband has stifled her personality for most of her adult life. Her husband is now fighting a chronic illness and she takes care of him twenty-four hours a day. Throughout the twenty-three years, she has grown to hate him. For the record, she didn't say that out loud. She does all the things she's supposed to do. She's staying with him, she takes care of him, she works two jobs to provide for the family, and she keeps it all together. On the inside, the bitterness towards him is eating her alive. She is blaming him for all of her problems. She feels trapped. She would love to walk away and end the marriage.

What she and people like her don't fully understand is that if she were to walk away, her problems would not go away. That's always the fallacy. Just change the circumstances! Get rid of these toxic people that are so needy! It doesn't work like that in real life. No matter where you go, there you are. You will take the bitterness with you, and until you face the condition of your heart, you will remain unhappy. My hubby Bob once said in a marriage conference, "Bitterness is like drinking poison hoping the *other* person will suffer and die."

Bitterness is like drinking poison hoping the other person will suffer and die.

I was able to clarify to this girl that even though she might think she just needed to drastically change her circumstances, the first step to true pleasure and freedom was to allow God to make changes her own heart.

The "Gardener" in this woman's life (God) wants to remove the over-bearing poisonous vines that are choking the life out of every other plant. I told her, "Begin by planting seeds of contentment, forgiveness, and unconditional love, nurturing and watering them with a revelation that God loves you. He really does! Enjoy God and let Him enjoy you. Unleash creativity and begin editing thoughts of despair. Choose life!"

Her eyes brimmed with tears as I asked her about the last time she created something...the last time she laughed while she was all alone…the last time she danced…she couldn't remember. I cried with her and said, "It's time to let yourself be who you were created to be. And it has nothing to do with leaving your husband, but loving yourself enough to find joy in your heart, and you'll effortlessly start loving those around you."

There are things that never should have happened to you. There's a good chance that people have planted bad seeds in your heart that have damaged you for years. There have been harsh and unkind words spoken to you that you have nurtured and you remember. They limit your dreams and squash your passion. I have no doubt that you have been hurt without cause, and those seeds that were planted are still alive and growing in your heart.

God Has a Happy Heart for You

We spoke to a man today who is completely miserable. He's in a new marriage to a wonderful woman, but he still hates his ex-wife so much that the anger seeps through into his present marriage. Not pretty! Hatred is a strong thing, and even justified, the bitterness definitely poisons your heart and steals every possibility that you'll ever really be happy. Would it help if he could punish his wife for what she truly deserves? Maybe logic would tell you that it would, but when it comes to heart issues, revenge is never satisfied; in fact, it just plants further seeds of rage and anger.

I want you to laugh easy. I want you to be free from fear of the future and fear of failure. I want you to dream again, belly laugh at least once a day, and dance like nobody's watching.

I want you to be able to put on all the songs you loved when you're a teenager and let God sing them over you.

Today is a great day to open your heart to possibilities. Maybe, just maybe you can finally let go of the inner-drive to change your circumstances, your kids, and God-probably-knows…your husband. My guess is that if you're anything like me, you've wasted day-loads of energy dreaming of how you can make changes in the world around you that will make you happy. Hmmm….a house-cleaner, a full-body massage once a week, effortless weight-loss, perfect children, loyal and fun friends, romance, and lots and lots of rest. Slightly unrealistic, but I'm sure you can relate to at least one of these. But I'm offering you something even better. I'm giving you the dream of a happy heart. It will change your life forever from the inside out. And you *will* start liking yourself!

A happy heart will change your life forever from the inside out. And you will start liking yourself!

There's a reason we live in vicious cycles. When we want change in our lives, our natural response is to make adjustments to our circumstances in the outside world. We try to muster our will power, gather our courage, and put a plan together. It works fine until we run out of steam. Then we get tired and fall into the same patterns as before. If we want to break the cycle of unhappiness, we're going to have to do something we have never done before. We must face the very core of who we are – our heart – and identify what's growing or even festering on the inside. Facing obstacles and ugliness in your own heart can be the scariest thing in your life – but absolutely the most rewarding in the end. God can break these cycles and transform our hearts!

The Power of Heart Transformation

Messages have been written on your heart since you were conceived in your mother's womb. Like seeds being planted, in most cases you didn't have a choice as to whether these messages were positive or negative. The messages turned into beliefs, and your life now reflects the beliefs you hold in our heart.

I am the third child born to my parents, after two brothers. I was cherished and adored and as a result I have always felt lovable and valuable. Even though I had a very positive upbringing, there have been debilitating beliefs that have affected my relationships. My personality is such that I have a strong need to please. I hate confrontation and being a disappointment in any way. It's just in the past ten years that I have understood the benefit of identifying these beliefs and replacing them with truth.

Being a "pleaser" has caused me to avoid truth and feel responsible to make everyone around me happy. The truth is that I no longer need to be afraid of confrontation because God's perfect love for me actually expels fear. I used to perform in my relationships, and even evade the truth if it would disappoint. I'm so thankful that God has journeyed with me to the places in my heart that were based on lies, and he will continue on this journey with me until I get to heaven one day.

Many people – and maybe you are one of them – have struggled with pretty serious rejection as children and have trouble trusting others. I have talked to some that didn't feel "wanted" as children, and were treated like they were more of a pain than a blessing to their family. Because their sense of value comes from deep in their heart, they don't believe they are valuable. Until they pull out this wrong belief they will feel unworthy and have difficulty receiving unconditional love.

Every single person is highly valuable. I have been making it my life quest the past several years to learn as much as I can about heart beliefs, and I have witnessed in my own life and others the power of doing "heart work." The lies and truth in our hearts affect the significant areas in our lives, as well as just little things like habits and daily behavior.

One of my best friends laughs at me because I compliment her for certain parenting skills she put in place, ones she did not think were a very big deal. We have similar personalities and we both had our children when we were barely twenty-one years old. But she did something I didn't do. As young as age three, her children were taught to wipe down the sink after washing their hands. The belief was written on their hearts: *Wiping down the sink is not an option. It is what we do.* Now, as her children are young adults this is natural behavior! It is automatic. They have been trained and they don't know anything different. They could be half asleep or in a bad mood but that will not change "who they are." Without even thinking they will keep that bathroom shiny.

Without being aware of it, I taught my kids what I felt was most important for them to know. Even though I love a clean house, teaching my kids to wipe down the sink was not on the top of my priority list! But now, her children have a belief written on their heart that my kids do not. Because her children believe deep in their hearts that this is not an option, they will always take the time to wipe down a sink. In fact, subconsciously, without even being fully aware, this is a practice that is put in place…set in stone! My children were not given this belief but it's never too late to learn!

This may seem like a silly example, but it is to show how beliefs are established in our sub-conscious, and then how we live out of our beliefs without any effort. I know a family in which both parents are physical education teachers. Since they could walk, their children have participated in sports and now as young adults they naturally live a life of fitness. They value their bodies and they look fantastic! As young adults, the kids wake up and find joy in grabbing their running shoes for a run. They make themselves a healthy balanced breakfast. The belief written on their heart is: *I am thankful for the body God has given me. I use it for optimum performance. I know that as I eat healthy and exercise and use my muscles I feel fantastic!* I don't think they think those thoughts; I think they live that way in "automatic" mode. For those of us where this belief was not established in our heart, we spend a lifetime trying to bring value to our bodies and fitness, but it's work. It takes more determination and self-control – behavior modification!

Another girl I know lives in utter chaos. You can hardly find a place to step in her apartment for fear of tripping over the clutter and mess. The first time I visited her, my mouth fell open in shock. All I could wonder is, "How does she find anything in here?" One of our mutual friends, out of love and devotion to her, spent an entire summer helping her reorganize her life. What a relief! The only disappointment is that within six months, it was just as messy and dirty as before.

The belief in her heart was: *It's not that important to pick that up right now. I'll do that later.* She wanted to change and live a new life, and she still can if she writes a new truth on her heart. We could teach her organizational skills till the cows come home. But if she establishes truth on her heart, the behavior, though deliberate at first, will become second nature.

You probably know situations about yourself that are coming to mind. Maybe you can see yourself in some of these scenarios. Possibly not the specifics, but there are areas in your life that you see a destructive cycle, and no matter who tries to come in and fix it for you, the only person capable of breaking the cycle is you, replacing the lies that are limiting your life, and replacing them with the truth of the provision of Jesus.

We can learn new habits and try to change our behavior, but our new habits will only last as long as our determination and self-will keeps them going. I'd guess that if you're tired, you might make it a week. However, learning to write truth on your hearts will change you from the inside out, making transformation effortless.

God is Glad You are Alive!

I can't help but think of our little guy, Robert. He is fully aware of our marriage story and has often heard us describe the crisis we went through when we first found out we were having a baby. By the time Robert was five, our first book, *Marriage*

Under Cover, was becoming popular and we were counseled to give an explanation to Robert before someone else told him how he was conceived. My challenge was to tell him about the affair and pregnancy while protecting his innocence. Not an easy task! While lying next to Robert one morning I asked, "Honey, you know how you are so much younger than your brothers and sister?" He said, "Yeah…" "And you know how you have hair and skin that is darker than the other kids?" He said, "Yeah…" "Well, that's because you came in a different way…" His reply was, "What part of you did I come out of?" Okay, that didn't work. End of conversation!

Learning to write truth on your hearts will change you from the inside out, making transformation effortless.

Take two. Several weeks later, Robert and I were reading a mother-and-son devotional book together and there were questions at the end of each chapter. The first question was for the mom to tell her son of a time when she made a big mistake and describe how God forgave her. Well, this was my moment. I told Robert that even though I loved Daddy very much, there was a time many years before that I kissed a man that wasn't Daddy, and that's how I ended up pregnant with him. Robert started crying, struggling to grasp that his mom made such a big mistake. I reassured him that Daddy forgave me, Jesus forgave me, and that God turned our story into a very happy ending, including him!

Robert fully understood the ramifications of what took place, and we cried and hugged and talked for about an hour. He asked many questions, and I called out to Bob to come and join us as we worked through the answers in attempt to communicate peace to any of the confusion he was experiencing. At the end of our conversation, it became obvious that he felt settled in his heart. We smiled with a sighs of relief as he threw his head back on the pillow and exclaimed, "Well, I'm sure glad I'm alive!"

It was just a few months later that he traveled with us to Brazil and heard us tell our marriage story about thirty times in twenty-one days. Each time Bob would tell the audience about the moment Robert was born and proclaim, "When my son was born, I gave him my name. I didn't want our son to ever wonder one day in his life whose boy he is! Would you like to meet him?" The crowd cheered every time as Robert ran up on stage from the front row and hugged his daddy's neck, and they held each other in a long embrace.

The power of that picture shows the power of how God can take a story with no possible happy ending and rescue and redeem it. Just last year on Robert's eighth birthday, Robert asked me if my parents had planned to have me. I said, "Yes, I think so!" "Oh," was his reply, "I guess you're not quite as special as me. I was born straight out of the heart of God." Robert knows his intrinsic value, and I can tell he likes himself. He's naturally happy and has zeal for each day.

You were not just brought into this world as a result of two people making love and conceiving a child. Just like Robert, no matter what circumstances surrounded your moment of conception, the truth is that you were born out of God's heart and brought into this world at the perfect time. Your life is meant to be.

Tranformation of Your Feelings

Having a healed and happy heart results in effortless joy that is immune from circumstances and people who disappoint you. Sometime your feelings may get in the way. It's so easy to live by our feelings thinking that they are the truth. However, feelings are only responders to our *interpretation* of what is happening around us. Feelings often do not represent the truth – at least the truth as it is from God's perspective. This is why it's so important to be full of God and have God's perspective so we can know the truth and it can set us free. Then when there is a conflict between our feelings and the truth, we need to follow the truth so we can change our feelings. In the end, you will always follow your predominant feelings. Influencing our heart to believe truth will change your feelings, thus changing your life.

What negative emotions are robbing you of joy and peace? Are you willing to ask God to help you identify the lie that is at the root of each negative emotion? I love the satisfaction of pulling out a weed and getting the *whole* thing, right down to those scraggly little ends. It takes some work to get to the very root of a negative emotion, just like pulling a big and established weed. Ask yourself what the negative emotion is, then get deeper and deeper by continually asking "Why?"

Take anger for example: You are easily angered by your husband. *Why?* He doesn't meet your expectations. *Why?* Because he's a jerk. (Stop! This exercise is about you so be careful not to blame others or circumstances if you want to get to the root.) Start again: *Why:* He doesn't meet your expectations. *Why?* Because he is supposed to make me happy and safe and provide for me. BINGO! You found the root, the lie you believe. You believe that your spouse is responsible for your happiness and should be your source of protection and provision.

Replace that with the truth: *Only God can be your source. Never a person.* Write this truth on your heart in first person. Mediate on it, repeat it, write it on cards all over your home and make it your creed: *Thank you God that I can trust you to be my Joy, my Provider, and my Protector.* Does this mean your husband is off the hook? No, you are in partnership. Each spouse *contributes* to the feelings that promote safety, provision, and joy for the other, but we cannot be each other's source. You're in charge of your part: Giving! But you have to stop giving him permission to steal the joy from your life. *Change you, not your husband.*

Remove the lie and plant the seed of truth, which is extreme trust in God. Now, nurture that seed by thinking, mediating, and feeling the emotions of joy and safety. Soon the world around you will come into alignment with the truth you are believing. It starts with you. It starts in the deepest place of your heart.

For several years I've been doing this exercise whenever a negative emotion arises. Sometimes it has taken months to persuade my heart of a certain truth. It has changed my thought life and eliminated mountains of stress. Try it. It takes work, but the reward is peace and joy.

If you want to learn more about heart transformation and heart work, I strongly recommend a program by Dr. Jim Richards called *Essential Heart Physics*. It's a four-week intensive with a daily plan that takes about thirty minutes a day. It's personally one of the best investments I've ever made. (This and other resources are available at www.bobandaudrey.com.

Dealing with your negative emotions instead of accepting them as normal will begin the process of "heart work." And identifying your desires helps you to get to know yourself. The About You section will help you begin the heart work God wants to do and the Medidate exercise is profound in discovering the truth about your heart.

about you

- What negative emotion do you want to get rid of first. Anger? Fear? Worry? Disappointment? Shame? Guilt?

- Ask God to identify the root, which is the disempowering belief that is etched in your heart. Do this by doing the "Why?" exercise I talked about in this chapter.

- Establish the empowering truth that you will use to replace the lie.

- Meditate and persuade your heart of the truth. Use your imagination to feel the results.

meditate

- What would you ask for if you could have absolutely anything?

- How would having those things make you feel? (Be detailed.)

- Remind yourself that God can make you feel those things without magically changing your circumstances, but rather by transforming your heart.

chapter 8

∞

removing hindrances to full-on happiness

Carrying around extra weight is not fun. This chapter is not about a number on your scale, but identifies seven "weights" that can slow you down when it comes to loving your life.

Are you ready to get rid of the weights that keep you from frolicking through life with a skip in your step? Why carry around extra stuff when you don't have to? This is our day to lighten our load and expend energy where it's going to result in the rewards you really want. The Bible has some excellent advice on how to live a life of extreme purpose:

Let us strip off every weight that slows us down, especially the sin that so easily trips us up. And let us run with endurance the race God has set before us.[19]

I love this! God not only wants to get sin out of the way, He also wants us to strip! That is, get rid of the stuff that "slows us down." In this chapter we'll identify and deal with seven hindrances or "weights" so that you can run the race God has for you...and win!

1. REMOVE SELF-DESTRUCTION – KNOW YOUR WORTH AND ACCEPT YOURSELF

Let's deal with the damage. Maybe you don't like yourself simply because there's so much *not* to like. Maybe you've hit vicious cycles where you want to change how you view yourself, but when you get tired or stop trying, your mind goes back into default mode and the self-destruction re-starts. It's tempting to believe you'll never change because history doesn't lie, and even though you make a new plan and set new goals, you end up exactly where you started.

Self-destruction is rooted in self-hatred. I realize that sounds harsh, but unfortunately this is not uncommon, especially for women who have put themselves under tremendous pressure to look and act a certain way and have experienced rejection and extreme disappointment. When you speak badly to yourself over a long period of time, you can actually become an expert at finding creative ways to torture yourself, to the degree that the punishment becomes an avenue of comfort. It sounds twisted, but these are the types of cycles that need to be broken once and for all.

If you are sensitive to guilt and have experienced shame and humiliation, it's common to involve yourself in secret behavior including throwing up, chewing your nails, depriving yourself of food, drinking alone, and feeling like you're not good enough. It's time to accept yourself, including your weaknesses and your strengths. You are not alone in this struggle.

When I speak publicly at women's events and tackle the issue of self-hatred, at least 80 percent of the women represented can relate to these thoughts. It can be scary to admit, but we can receive some comfort knowing that many women are experiencing similar pain.

When you speak badly to yourself over a long period of time, you can actually become an expert at finding creative ways to torture yourself, to the degree that the punishment becomes an avenue of comfort.

There is something uniquely beautiful about you that no one else in the world shares. God knew you before you were even conceived! He will always pursue you in love, so that you will know how, through Jesus, there is forgiveness. He is definitely not holding your sins against you.

Whether you believe Jesus or not, it doesn't change His thoughts towards you. You are completely loved and accepted, without changing one thing. It is my hope and prayer that you will align your life with God's love and love yourself as He loves you.

It doesn't take a certain personality type to develop a healthy relationship with yourself. I have seen every type of person, every size, every shape and every culture completely overcome the lie that they are unlovable. Anyone and everyone can experience miraculous transformation.

Loving myself has brought me to a place of accepting the way God made me. I suspect every woman has something they would love to change about themselves. Our behavior, outbursts, and mistakes have made it easy for people to reject and abandon us. We begin to believe that we have to completely change who we are in order to be loved. It's honorable and effective to change behavior, but there are some things that are part of you that will never change – so let's accept ourselves as we are!

God Likes How You Look

Let's nail a big one: our physical appearance. Sure, some would think talking about physical appearance is shallow, but it's a big deal in our image-conscious culture that quickly judges our flaws. This culture can cause us to be very hard on ourselves. For the first half of my life I hated my big nose and big butt. I thought about how much I would love to change them, and this obsessive thinking brought too much attention to my "downfalls." Instead of thanking God for the way He made me, I concentrated on what He could have done different. What was He thinking?

When our little girl Janelle was three years old, she was in the bathroom with me as I was getting ready to go out. Still naked, I had stepped out of the shower and was applying makeup. As I leaned forward to clearly see the mirror, Janelle suddenly started patting my butt with both hands and said, "Mommy you have a really big bum." I said, "I know! Do you think you'll have a big bum like me when you're a mommy?" She replied, "I sure hope so!" So funny!

Loving ourselves starts with what pair of glasses we are using. Judging ourselves becomes a bad habit. A little piece of trivia – Janelle is in her twenties now and did *not* inherit my – let's say – extra shapely body-type! She wears those little boy-jeans and I think, "Who did she get that butt from?" She has that disease I like to call, "Noassatall." And I have come to love the fact that I am abundant when it comes to junk in the trunk and I'm just going to "work it-work it!"

Two weeks ago I met a beautiful girl in her early twenties in New Zealand. I instantly noticed her radiant smile and twinkly-eyes. She told me her story of how she absolutely hated her freckles. I listened to her heart as I looked at her gorgeous face that was absolutely covered in freckles – more than I had ever seen. She told me that Jesus spoke to her heart one day and revealed that each freckle was a kiss from Him. Both of us instantly had tears in our eyes as we acknowledged how loved she is. I said, "Girl, he couldn't *stop* kissing you…" She said, "I know!"

It's taken many years, but I have not only accepted the way God made me, but thank him for each unique and precious part. He didn't create any one of us haphazardly, but with love and creativity He knitted us together in our mother's womb, exactly as he saw fit.[20] I wish I could meet you in person right this minute, squeeze you and celebrate how beautiful you are. Probably the best thing to do right now would be to smile right where you are (I'm not kidding) and say, "Thank you Jesus, that you call me beautiful…" It might even make you cry because you've never received those words, or because you haven't believed them. But it's a giant leap towards accepting yourself and recognizing the beauty God gave you.

Know your Worth

It's impossible to truly like ourselves if we don't know our inherent worth and understand the treasure that we are in God's eyes. One of the quickest ways to measure how you feel about yourself is to evaluate your ability to *receive*. Receiving is an art within itself. Children typically receive effortlessly without question! They are uninhibited and trusting. They don't wonder if there are "strings attached" or what the motive of the giver could be. Children typically receive love, attention, gifts, and admiration with smiles and joy, not even considering whether or not they deserve it. And without effort, reciprocate that love!

As adults however, our sense of worth has been violated through hurt and pain. We experience rejection, betrayal, and broken promises. Our heart is not convinced that we deserve the very best.

I firmly believe that God has given us gifts that are sitting right in front of us with our names on them, yet we refuse to open them. The finished work of Jesus Christ entitled us to an inheritance that is incomprehensible. If I have perfect health; no fear, guilt, or shame; an ability to be creative, purposeful, and prosperous; with an abiding emotion of being perfectly loved, I would say I have it all. The Bible says I have all of these things, so what lie am I holding onto that prevents me from receiving my inheritance?

Agree With Your Worth

The key that unlocks the power of receiving is agreeing with your worth in God your Creator. Last year we had very fun Christmas party for our ministry staff where we played several silly games that brought roars of laughter. One of the games was called Santa's Beard. Each team chose a person who would smother their face in petroleum jelly and then stuff it into a large bowl full of cotton balls. The person with the most cotton balls stuck to their "beard" won the event. My dad had everyone in hysterics as he spontaneously peeled off his shirt so he wouldn't have to worry about the massive amounts of petroleum jelly on his face and neck.

God's solutions, provision, and unconditional love have a limitless supply (like the cotton balls). But these blessings only "stick" to someone who *receives* them; they do not stick to those who do not feel their personal worth and value. Worth and value is the glue that holds onto the gift given. The only way we will know our worth is simply to believe what God says about us.

By faith we trust He is telling us the truth. Let me tell you the truth about you: You are completely loved by Him. He is not disappointed in you, but is pursuing you with His forgiveness and grace. In fact He is crazy about you – He knows what makes you smile, He knows the desires of your heart and He wants a relationship with you that is real without an ounce of religion or rules attached to it. When you believe and are completely

The only way we will know our worth is simply to believe what God says about us.

convinced that this is true, your heart will be transformed and you will begin opening the presents that have been there for you this whole time.

When Bob and I speak at marriage conferences, one of the "intimacy exercises" we teach the participating couples is what we call, "I Love You – Thank You." Couples are asked to face each other and gaze deeply into each other's eyes. The man starts and says, "I love you." The woman's usual response would be, "I love you too," but we change things up and ask that she take time to *receive* and acknowledge the love spoken to her, and then thank him for his love. So, she responds, "Thank you." Then she says, "I love you," and he says, "Thank you." Sounds simple, but this is a profound lesson in receiving. For only one minute couples take time to receive each other's love. The effects of this simple and short exercise when done regularly will foster intimacy and communicate worth to each other's hearts.

This also works with God. Let's try this exercise with Him. The Bible says:

> See how very much our Father loves us, for he calls
> us his children, and that is what we are![21]

God loves you. Listen to Him in the quiet place in your heart say, "I love you… and I like being with you too." Respond to Him right now and say, "Thank you."

Bob would be the first to tell you about his battle with worthlessness. We have been married nearly twenty-seven years, and I have seen the love of God melt his heart as he receives God's truth about his value and worth. The more He understands and receives worth from his heavenly Father, the more he is able to receive love from me.

I met a young girl in New York a few weeks ago and told her the premise of this book. She said, "I used to have a boy-friend that didn't like himself, and it was impossible to compliment him or communicate love to him! It's frustrating when people can't receive love! I'm so glad you're helping people to like themselves."

Worthlessness is a huge battle for most people, and God has given all of us an opportunity to help others understand their value and worth. But we can't give away something we don't have. As God downloads His view of us – one full of unconditional love, acceptance, and worth – and we receive it, we are then able to contribute to the worth of others. We communicate their value through respecting their ideas, appreciating their gifts and talents, cheering on their dreams, and stopping all nit-picking and complaining about their shortcomings.

I clearly remember a time when our daughter Janelle seemed a little down. I wanted to encourage her heart, and as I walked by the couch I intended to touch her and tell her I love her. As I approached her, God nudged my heart and said, "Tell her: 'Thank you for loving *me* so much – you're so good at it!'" I did just that, and immediately peace rested on her and she smiled and said, "You're welcome!" It was exactly what she needed. I received love from her in that moment. I presumed I should walk by and communicate my love for her, but God knew that she needed to be encouraged and affirmed that she is great at loving her mama!

Knowing Your Worth Is Simply Knowing *God*

God wants to communicate how He feels about you and how valuable you really are to Him. Receiving became intentional to me during a worship service I was in years ago. I began to realize that most church songs had to do with our love and devotion to God, expressing our undying commitment. That's all good, in fact it's very good! But the Lord gently asked me, "When is it My turn to sing over you?" What a concept! The particular love song being sung was full of love, and I closed my lips and opened the ears of my heart. I heard Him sing the same song to me.

Tears streamed down my face. With a childlike heart, I believed His words to me and received them. Since that time, He sings over me regularly. I often listen to my favorite love songs from Junior High and I let myself get lost in hearing Him sing these songs to me. You may think I'm crazy, but the other day I was listening to Andy Gibb sing "I just wanna be your everything" on my iPhone and I received it as a song directly from Jesus to me.

There is a whole lot of giving and receiving going on in my relationship with God – and the best part is, He is the One who created me. He knows every one of my intricate thoughts and desires. He has my best interest in mind and will always be my compass showing where to turn, what to say, and who to talk to. He will help me in my relationships, my health, and my dreams. Loving Him is definitely not work – it comes as natural as breathing.

Having time alone with Him could never be described as a discipline when it's something I crave more than food and drink. And I know He meets me and understands me. I have learned to receive from Him, and I continue to be challenged to receive more. I know I have only tapped the tip of the iceberg, and He has more in store for me than eyes have ever seen, ears have heard, or mind could imagine.[22]

It's significant for me that He has redeemed these particular songs from when I was young, because it was during puberty that my love was awakened and I had desire for attention from the opposite sex. I made choices to look for love in all the wrong places as I reveled in boys noticing me and wanting me. God is not limited by time, and as I listen to the songs of those times, He takes me back and heals my heart. As I hear the love songs, I bask in the attention He gives me and He restores my innocence and purity. Truth is being established on my heart: *He is the One who fully satisfies me and pursues me with an everlasting and romantic love.*[23]

Every girl wants romance – that is a God-given desire! I don't try and squash this desire, and I don't unrealistically demand my husband to rush to my every whim and fleeting wish. Instead I enjoy God as my Bridegroom. The Bible clearly tells us that there is a wedding feast planned and the body of Christ is His bride. And we, the body of Christ, are His bride. I have a unique place in His body (and so do you). There are secrets and smiles we share that only He and I experience.

During a board game last Christmas with our kids and their friends, we were asked what we love most about our mothers.

Our daughter Janelle said, "I love that my mom knows me. She knows me better than any other person. She knows what I need before I even ask, and she always understands." I was honored by her response. This is how God is with us: He knows us better than any other person. He knows what we need even before we ask.

When teaching at marriage conferences, Bob and I take time to have fun describing the differences between men and women. We like to give great advice about how to love each other in a way that is "received." Bob baits the audience with the question, "Do you know the most romantic thing you could ever do for your wife?" The men scramble to get their pens and papers out because invariably almost every one of them feels like a failure in this area! He then reveals a surprising (and inexpensive!) answer when he says, "Get to know her." All the women take a deep breath and sigh.

How loved we feel when our men continue to explore our thoughts and feelings and seek out the treasure that is in us! After twenty-six years of marriage, I still get shivers when Bob gazes deep in my eyes and searches my heart for new expressions of beauty and mentions something he has recently noticed about me and loves about me.

The Bible says that God does the same thing: He looks deeply into our hearts and knows us intimately. He knows where you are and everything you do. He knows every thought. He even knows what you are going to say before you say it. [24] How's that for intimacy! This intimate knowing says one thing: *You are valuable and worth knowing.*

But it all starts with receiving. The Bible says that those who should have received Jesus did not. However, "as many as received Him, to them He gave the right to become children of God, to those who believe in His name."[25] Knowing your worth is all about receiving what you need to from God Himself – from the start of your relationship with Him until you see Him face to face.

about you

- Think about how pressured you feel to look and act a certain way. How healthy is it?

- Are you able to receive compliments? Why or why not?

- How often do you question your value and worth? Do you remember when this started?

meditation

Get some index cards and create truth tablets. Feel free to make them personal, but here is a guideline: Put these in places where you'll read them!

- God calls me beautiful and loves me completely.

- God is not disappointed in me.

- God knows what makes me smile.

- God calls me His treasure.

- There is nobody just like me.

- I am valuable and important.

2. REMOVE UNNEEDED SERIOUSNESS
LAUGH AT YOURSELF

Our favorite memories usually include special occasions, tender moments, or plain-old laughing-our-heads-off. Laughing is powerful, energizing, and necessary, and this includes laughing at ourselves. We all have ample opportunities to laugh at ourselves, and if this isn't a natural skill for you, it is something you can choose to learn. Instead of taking yourself so seriously, when you laugh it invites others to laugh with you and brings healing to situations and circumstances that could otherwise be humiliating.

Some of my most endearing memories include belly laughing with Bob, our children, our friends, and family. I'm thankful that I am easily amused and laugh loud and easily. It doesn't take much to get me going! I've heard that a true comedian doesn't laugh at his or her own jokes. If that's the case, there is no way that I could be a comedian. Some things I do are funny every time, and I can't keep myself from enjoying every opportunity for a good laugh.

If you find that you haven't laughed enough lately, make a decision to see the lighter side of life and even ask God for help in this area. When praying for couples regarding their marriage, I easily discern when there hasn't been enough fun in the relationship. When I ask them about it, they often both get tears in their eyes when they confess they can't remember the last time they had a belly laugh together. I suggest to them that they pray and ask God for funny stuff to happen, and the ability to laugh when it does. God cares about this area of your life. He created laughter. Think about it. He didn't have to, He wanted to!

Years ago when we had three children between the ages of nine and thirteen, we traveled many miles to visit my grandma. She has since passed away, but I have extraordinary memories of her in my life until I was forty-three years old. My favorite thing about her was the fact that she prayed for Bob and I and our children every day. I mean *every* day. I believe we are continuing to live in God's favor and grace

Ask God for funny stuff to happen, and the ability to laugh when it does. God cares about this area of your life. He created laughter.

(and will continue to do so for generations to come) as a result of my praying grandma! This definitely inspires me to be one of those grandmas who visits God's throne room of grace each day on behalf of my clan!

On this one particular visit we arrived in her apartment and quickly noticed a mountain of 4x6 plastic photo albums on her coffee table. If you're too young to remember the pre-digital days, you could develop a roll of film and put all the pictures in an album to share with others. Now our phones and other electronic devices do the trick!

Anyway, I come from a large family and have many incredible cousins. Between aunts, uncles, nephews, cousins, etc., there were probably eighty of these little books. I began rummaging through them, beginning to feel like a loser for neglecting to send my grandma pictures of our little family. I couldn't seem to find one featuring the Meisners, until…

I opened an album and immediately gasped with joy and pride as I saw Christopher, aged two on the first page. Gorgeous! I continued through the little pages and found shots of my huge pregnant belly, expecting Janelle. The bliss came to a halting cringe as I turned the page to see a close up of Janelle being born. Yes, it's exactly what you're thinking. I'm on a hospital bed, my legs are wide open and Janelle's head is about to come out. Then there was a close up of her body being born. The next shot was especially precious as she was warmly laid on my naked breast. Oh! The first drink from my nipple – can't miss that one! I literally lost my breath as the reality hit me that this photo album had been on Grandma's coffee table for about ten years! We obviously put together two photo albums, one for Grandma, and one for our very-extremely-private stash for no one but Bob and I to see. The wrong one got sent to Grandma! For years my relatives have been scoping those albums and nobody confiscated the evidence! I couldn't believe it!

You can guarantee that I took that photo album home with me, but then had to confront the humiliation of knowing that probably every uncle, nephew, and cousin had a full-frontal view of my va-jay-jay. Not exactly comforting. Go ahead and feel sorry for me at this point, please. This is about as shocking and inappropriate as a girl could get. I had a choice to make. I could either hide under sunglasses and a huge hat at the next family reunion over this embarrassingly scandalous album, or I could throw back my head and laugh at myself. I chose the latter. Don't feel sorry for me at all. Rather laugh at such incriminating circumstances! In "hindsight" those pictures should never have been taken in the first place (no pun intended).

Maybe your mouth is still hanging open and you just can't imagine laughing at yourself at such a humiliation. Laughing at yourself is often characteristic to non-self-conscious personalities, but it is also a learned behavior. It's a choice. Taking ourselves too seriously and getting super-sensitive robs us of laughter and joy in our life. And choosing joy is something God compels us to do. Scriptures say to "Rejoice in the Lord always – again I say rejoice!"[26] and "The joy of the Lord is our strength."[27] Let joy become the abiding emotion of your life.

The Difference Between Serious and Intentional

I'm just not so important that I have to be serious all the time. I recently had the awe-inspiring revelation of the difference between getting serious, and getting intentional. I can be full of joy on the edge of silly, and still be extremely intentional about my life's purpose, what I do in a day, and my relationship with God and my family.

At about the same time you stop laughing at yourself and life is when you can get extremely introspective. It used to happen to me far too often! For example, I would meet a bunch of people, have the time of my life, but notice that one person didn't like me or "take to me." Did I go home thinking about the blessing of finding heaps of new friends? No, I thought about that one person who didn't like me. The fear of failure in me said, "I wonder what I did to offend her? I wonder what part of my personality she doesn't like? Maybe it's my obnoxious laugh…" and the thoughts would continue. When things went differently than what I had hoped, I reverted to being self-absorbed and made it all about me. I also punished myself with insults trying to figure out what I did wrong.

I'm a huge advocate of learning during times of pain and facing weaknesses head-on, but it doesn't take massive amounts of introspection. Learning these lessons takes some time alone, quiet in my secret place with God. It is there that I ask him questions, allow Him to examine my heart and find if there is any evil in my heart, and gently remove any lies I have believed. I am definitely a work in progress and want to be extremely teachable, but the people who dislike me and don't understand me are not the ones who need to be my teachers. My Daddy in heaven who loves me…now there's someone I'll learn from!

So we can be intentional about learning the lessons that God has for us in life without getting overly introspective and serious – to the point of losing the joy God has for us each day.

Joy Can Help You

There is something very amazing about joy that helps us get through life. The Bible says:

When troubles come your way, consider it an opportunity for great joy. For you know when your faith is tested, your endurance has a chance to grow. So let it grow. For when your endurance is fully developed you will be perfect and complete lacking nothing.[28]

The kingdom of God is righteousness, peace, and **joy**![29] One of the fruits of the Holy Spirit is **joy**.[30] God has joy for you, and one great way to walk in this joy each day is to drop unnecessary seriousness and take time to laugh at yourself.

about you

- Do you laugh at yourself easily? Explore why this may be challenging for you.

- What are a few things you can do to help you not take life so seriously? Be as specific and situational as possible.

meditation

- Recall a memory when something funny happened to you. Share it with a friend!

3. REMOVE REGRET – FAIL FORWARD[31]

Bob and I have had the opportunity of ministering in Scotland and had a day off to enjoy the sites. It was a glorious day of touring, learning history, and visiting castles. Our final destination was the castle where the movie *Braveheart* was filmed. I looked forward to the stunning beauty of green fields. We arrived at sunset and I wasn't disappointed. Everything I saw was picturesque and stunning. The only problem was that we arrived after the castle was officially closed. No big deal, except I had to use the bathroom.

Without drawing attention to my problem, I mentioned to Bob and the group that I was going for a little "walk" by myself. I grew up camping with two brothers and have absolutely no issues with using a bush if I need to. Two of the Scottish women offered to come with me and we opened a huge, creaky steel gate that led to the cemetery. We walked down the path until I spotted the perfect place to go number one. There was a large abandoned structure with a narrow walking path next to it, made private by a huge hedge of greenery. It provided a private, peaceful spot for me to do my business. The two women offered to stand guard as I did what I needed to do. As I relieved myself, I began looking at the hedge right next to me. There were assorted green leaves, and because I didn't have a tissue, I began examining which leaf would suffice as a substitute for toilet paper. I eyed a big round flat one that would be perfect. I finished and in one swoop ripped the leaf off the bush and wiped myself. Instantly I screamed uncontrollably. The little woman guarding the entrance gasped in her sweet

Scottish accent, "You didn't use the nettles, did you?" Oh, is that what just happened? Teeny-tiny invisible stinging nettles covered my fingers and, that's right, let's call it my "area." For several hours I walked with my legs apart, hoping and praying that the pain would subside. It did. I'm fine. It was simply a stupid mistake.

Let's apply this to life. You make a choice that brings pain to your life. It wasn't intentional and it's not morally wrong, it was just not smart. What do you do now? It's impossible to get the "nettles" out and often it happens in the most private areas of your life. Things you can't share with just anyone. And no one could possibly understand the pain and discomfort!

We have all done stupid stuff…things that are much more serious than Scottish nettles. We have wasted time doing ridiculous things, we have invested money and lost it, and we have neglected and abused relationships that are now dead and gone. If there were a great reason to be mad at yourself, any of these would have enough evidence for sorrow and regret. The thing about regret is that there are no do-overs. What's done is done. And sometimes there are consequences.

Learn to Let It Go

To "fail forward" means that you allow failure to move you forward in life instead of stunt your growth or stop the forward progress. Learning from our mistakes is what develops character in us and can—if we let it—become a step-

Learning from our mistakes is what develops character in us and can—if we let it—become a stepping-stone toward something better.

ping-stone toward something better. But once we have learned what we need to learn, we need to let it go and stop beating ourselves up – stop dwelling on it and giving it attention.

Just last night we were having dinner with my parents and they told us about a coffee cup with the inscription, "Don't look back unless it makes you smile." My mom said, "At age seventy-two it's easy to think of all the things I could have done different. But we are refusing to do that, and only think of the things that make us smile." I saw my parents exchange a loving smile with each other when they talked about it. This sounds like a light, feel-good moment, but it's more than that; they have been extremely intentional about making this a lifestyle. We can choose to live without regret.

Don't look back unless it makes you smile.

Bob and I have made some financial investments that have cost us huge amounts of money. The home we are living in now is worth half of what we bought it for, and subsequently has cost us our life savings. In hindsight, would we have done things differently? Of course! What have I learned through this? I have persuaded my heart of the truth that trumps the facts. The fact is, at this moment, we don't have a lot of wealth. The truth is that trusting in wealth is not true security.[32] Therefore, I am learning the security and freedom of knowing God as my provider in every way. It is His pleasure to prosper us, so I want to have my heart in line with His, and will believe that He desires to benefit me and prosper every part of my life. I am set up and ready for His success in every way, knowing that He is my source. I will never lack the finances to do everything He has purposed me to do. I have learned a lot through my mistakes, but I don't spend time dwelling on the wrong decision, thus defaming my character.

I know people who are in mourning simply because of lost time. They wasted years of their lives, investing in someone or something, or some dream that didn't prove fruitful. One of our sons was going through this last year and I said, "Honey, don't think of it as wasted time because now you know, beyond a shadow of a doubt, what you don't want to do with your life!" Looking ahead with hope and a transformed heart will set you up for a bright tomorrow. God gives us the gift of a new day as we wake up to His mercies that are new every morning.[33] Bob and I wrote a book entitled, *The Gift of a New Day* that talks about new motivation and a new outlook on life. God loves to make things new!

Avoid Regret Through Humility

The most difficult regrets are the ones that involve relationships. All of us have mismanaged vital relationships, the most important being family. Maybe you've been divorced, maybe you have estranged children, or maybe you're not on speaking terms with your precious family. Be the first one to move towards reconciling the relationship by not holding the other person's wrongdoing against them. Instead of wondering when that other person is going to make things right, make the first move yourself. Don't remind them of their shortcomings, but rather refuse to be defensive and just tell them any mistakes *you* have made.

The best way to avoid regret in life is through humbling our-selves and choosing others as more important than ourselves. Offering radical forgiveness does not make you a doormat, but rather a person of dignity who will fight for reconciliation and lay down your own rights for the sake of another. It's not an issue of being right. Even if you are right, you don't have to defend your position. The Bible says,

> Don't be selfish; don't try to impress others. Be humble, thinking of others as better than yourselves.[34]

I recently spoke in length with a woman who relayed the following story. She was the assistant to her pastor for many years, covering for his shortcomings and bringing energy and motivation to church projects. In her loneliness and desperation for escape she involved herself in an affair. The pastor found out and let her go. She is now an "outcast," adding to her sin and shame, and the pastor is left with a confused church fam-ily. Now, neither people are speaking to each other, dismissing years of relationship. Instead of seeing how she had hurt him, she held huge amounts of bitterness against him. Her unspo-ken expectation was that the pastor should express appreciation and recognition for what she had done for her church for all of those years. His expectation was that she show sorrow for what she did to him and the church. I know for a fact that the pas-tor doesn't have any idea of the pain he inflicted and wouldn't even know to apologize. So what advice should I give the girl I'm sitting with?

I said to her, "I know you feel angry and hurt, but he does too. But instead of punishing him, the best gift you can give yourself is be the first one to bring reunion. Ask that he forgive you for the hurt you caused."

She said "That would almost impossible."

"I understand," I said, "but that very step will set you free and you'll be able to sleep at night again."

When there's a rift in a relationship, there's a *very* high chance that you have also hurt the person who has hurt you. You may not know what you have done to that person to hurt them. If you do, ask them to forgive you. If you don't, approach them and simply say, "By your actions and words towards me, I detect that I have hurt you in some way. Can you help me understand what I have done?" There's a good possibility that as you go and ask for forgiveness, the other person won't just quietly forgive you and move on, but will rather want to make sure you *know* what you did to hurt them. They might have a need to punish you and tell you off. It's happened to me. Without defending yourself, let that person continue. It's hard to let someone tell you off without defending yourself; in fact, it's impossible unless you know your worth in God. I have experienced restored relationships by simply asking forgiveness and laying down the right to be right.

When it comes to doing stupid stuff, sometimes there is a mess to clean up. Most of the time we can't undo our mistakes, get back the time or money we have wasted, or the times we have hurt and mistreated others. However, we can deal with the lies we have believed in our heart that have fueled our thinking and caused us to make the mistake in the first place.

Liking yourself means you courageously learn from mistakes and refuse to live with regret. God did not design you to carry around baggage of regret. Please give yourself a break. Even though I live with the consequences of past, wrong choices, I refuse to dwell on them and punish myself. Embrace your mistakes and the choices that have caused you pain and start new. Don't look back unless it makes you smile.

about you

- With whom do you need to mend a relationship? What first step can you make to do this?

- What regrets do you find yourself remembering?

meditation

- Think of some mistakes that you have made. Consider what valuable lessons you have learned and how this knowledge can help you positively in the future.

- Now, when the memory comes up, refuse to dwell on it!

4. REMOVE FEAR – RECEIVE LOVE

A couple of days ago I recognized fear in my life *again*. We all have tendencies towards core fears that we have to conquer continuously. The great news is that if we refuse to accept fear as normal, we can learn to identify it quickly and choose perfect love.

In my recent case, I didn't recognize fear immediately. Fear is sometimes sneaky! Others around us can probably smell it from miles away, but we get comfortable with it and don't even notice the paralyzing power it has on our lives. Because of an overwhelming work schedule, I began to panic and wonder how I would meet deadlines. For several days, fear of failure fueled my days. There were impossible tasks ahead, so I subconsciously administrated adrenaline into my system, and decided to face the impossible feats on my own. Let's just say I get highly determined, maybe a celebrated characteristic from some standards, but not in line with God being my Source.

A couple of days I woke up about two hours too early. Instead of tackling work, I am thankful to report that I intentionally got in touch with God. I forced myself to stop thinking about the work I had to get done and talked to Jesus about my heart. His peace enveloped me, and that's when I recognized the fear of failure that I had given into the past week. God didn't point His finger at me and judge me for my craziness, but rather smiled and invited me to let Him take the driver's seat. I happily confirmed my trust in Him, and the fear of the future, and the fear of failure was instantly expelled as I received God's love.

Had I continued to operate from the place of fear, I most likely would have sabotaged my future in attempts to control the process. Fear will cause you to control. Fear raises its ugly head in so many areas:

- Fear of loss
- Fear that we won't have enough money to live
- Fear of failure
- Fear of the future
- Fear that we will be betrayed
- Fear that we will be rejected
- Fear of loneliness
- Fear that we will lose our children or those close to us
- Fear of pain and dying
- Fear of conflict
- Fear of getting fat
- Fear of sickness
- Fear of making decisions

Unfortunately, this list could go on long enough to fill several books. Isn't that sad? Even worry becomes normal within our thoughts, but it doesn't have to!

Worry is simply meditating on the worst possible outcome. The answer to fear is always love because God's perfect love expels all fear.[35] I am loved perfectly; therefore, I have nothing to fear. No matter how long you have lived with a particular fear, it no longer has to define you. Ask God to help you overcome the fear and learn everything you can about what He has to say about it.

Fear has the potential to sabotage your future, paralyze you from moving forward, and can make you difficult to live with. Remember: *Fear is a habit that can prevent us from living our dreams. Love yourself enough to face your fears.* Allow God to love you through the journey to wholeness. Making peace a priority sets you up for loving your life.

about you

- What fears are you battling against right now?
- What do you worry most about?

meditation

- Think about how you feel when you're at peace. Describe it.
- Consider how vast the love of God is. Pursue God's love to melt the fear and worry from your life.

5. REMOVE GREED – ENJOY WHAT YOU HAVE

Have you ever worked on a jigsaw puzzle, persevered through hours of paying attention to every intricate detail, anticipating the feeling of placing that last final piece, only to find out that the final piece is missing? The anti-climax takes away the joy of the journey and it almost feels like the entire project was a waste of time.

Our human nature compels us to focus on the one missing piece instead of the beauty of the entire puzzle. I have noticed this in my own "puzzle of life." I can have so many great things in my life to be thankful for, but instead I fixate on the thing I don't have.

God has given us all things to enjoy[36] and has made us complete in Him.[37] He never intended for us to be frustrated in life because one piece is missing and it's ruining the entire picture. God's character isn't one that He would give you everything you need except one thing in order to torture you. Even though our tendency is to focus on the missing piece, our life *isn't* a puzzle that we have to try and figure out. Life is a gift – a journey through time with our Creator in a thriving relationship and close communion. A giant leap toward liking ourselves is choosing to be content and realize that focusing on what's missing is actually torture. Last time I checked, torture is a very mean thing to do, and we are learning to be our own best friend! We would never harp on our best friend, reminding them of what they're missing.

Choosing contentment is saying a great big *No* to comparing yourself with others for the purpose of putting yourself down. We can learn from others, be inspired and influenced by others, admire others, and even notice what others have that we don't, as long as it motivates us from a place of hope and fulfilling dreams. We know we've crossed the line when we meditate on what someone has, knowing that we can't or won't ever have it, and that lack creates anger at ourselves.

You have everything you need because of what Jesus has done. He is pursuing you with an everlasting love that covers your weaknesses, which diminishes the feeling of lack in your life. Maybe you don't have the perfect kids, perfect body, perfect house, or perfect job, but the One who loves you is perfect, and He lives His life through you.[38]

Can you begin to feel the peace that surrounds contentment? Can you see how living a content life will assist you in your journey to liking yourself? Concentrate, meditate, and focus on everything you have; everything you love about your life; everything you're thankful for. Invite Jesus to help you to overcome any tendencies to compare and let the joy of the Lord fill your heart.

about you

- What's the "missing piece" in your life?

- Who do you compare yourself with? What do they have that you do not? Why is that so important to you?

- What do you like most about a contented life?

meditation

- Make a list of what you are thankful for. A really long list! Think of everything. Take time to read through the list, thanking God for even the smallest of things.

- Share your thanksgiving with another person. Notice how your thankfulness affects that person and inspires them to be thankful as well.

6. REMOVE SHAME – WALK IN FREEDOM

I remember a time that Bob and I shared our marriage story at a marriage conference and a gentleman came up to me after the meeting and asked, "Audrey, is it just like being an alcoholic? Is it 'once and alcoholic, always an alcoholic, once an adulterer, always an adulterer?'"

This language is adopted from the systematic twelve-step program that is a highly effective in getting clean from addictions. You may have heard a recovering alcoholic say, "I've been clean for twelve years." That is a huge milestone! However, I don't want to be identified as a "recovering adulterer" and simply be *clean* from ever doing that again. I want to be free! I want my daily victory to be effortless, and I don't want this "thing I did" to limit my future or identify me in any way. I don't want to be in bondage or be scared of appropriate friendships with men or think I'm some kind of a magnet to sexual indiscretions. Because of Jesus, I'm more than clean…I'm free!

From everything I've learned since the affair, the key to getting off-the-charts-freedom is to get rid of shame at the deepest heart level. I mentioned in the previous chapter that our heart is like a garden. If our heart is a garden, then shame is more than an entangling vine, but rather the soil in which many negative emotions and dysfunctional behavior rise and grow. Jesus paid the price to forgive our sins and take away every residue of shame. If you've ever had someone say to you, "Shame on you," it's time to say, "Shame *off* me!"

The Difference Between Guilt and Shame

Guilt and shame are very different. Feeling guilty about doing something wrong or hurting another person is an indicator – it's what helps us recognize that our conscience is alive and points to areas we need to make right. Therefore, guilt is not a bad thing; it's what you do in *response* to guilt in your life. I personally have lived with the weight of guilt and hate the thoughts and feelings that accompany it. I have not only learned to recognize it quickly, but make aggressive steps to do whatever it takes to make things right in my own heart, as well as in my relationships.

Here's what guilt can motivate you to do:

- Stop what you're doing
- Deal with the ramifications
- Tell the truth and face the consequences
- Stop destructive behavior

So why do we ignore the guilt?

- Fear of consequences
- Don't want to stop behavior – We somehow believe that the pleasure or escape of the behavior outweighs the pain it causes

If you are participating in sin (an activity that violates your moral code) and you feel guilty, my prayer is that you will let the guilt motivate you to face the consequences and stop the destructive behavior. If you're feeling guilty and you don't really know why, you are probably living under expectations from yourself and others that are not substantiated. People have most likely put on you responsibilities that were not yours to carry and have blamed you inappropriately. This isn't the time to get angry with them, but simply recognize where the guilt is coming from and put it in proper perspective. I have learned that I don't have to give people the permission or room to manipulate me with guilt and can refuse to receive it! When you feel guilty, it's pretty hard to like yourself.

Guilt says, "This is what you have done." Shame, on the other hand, says, "This is *who you are.*" It goes far beyond your actions and attacks your very worth and identity. Dr. Jim Richards describes it like this, "Shame is a negative emotion that controls your life by keeping you in constant awareness of your sin. Shame is what keeps you connected to your past. It insists that you define your life by your personal failures."

Jim is our dear friend and has taught us more about our heart from the biblical standpoint than anyone else. He says that our heart will do everything possible to affirm that which it believes is true. This means that if my heart is full of shame and believes that I am unworthy and undeserving, when I walk into a room or a situation, people will subconsciously agree with how I see myself.

Shame attracts judgment. I experienced this myself for a couple years after giving birth to Robert. My heart in essence would send out an invisible message: *Disqualified.* My thoughts toward myself were, "Audrey, you were so stupid to do this. You will never live this down. You have caused more pain to Bob and yourself than you were ever meant to bear. You'll never be trusted again. You'll forever be disqualified from true happiness." The shame kept me dwelling on my past sin and defining my life by my personal failures.

Living with these kinds of thoughts hugely affected my life. The result of living in shame is that I lived sub-standard to what Jesus had planned for me when He created me and placed me on this earth. I didn't laugh easily and I didn't have peace in my heart or mind. Our marriage was surviving, but not full of laughing and dreaming together. I found myself always trying harder to be better and earn a better life. In a nutshell, I was a tired survivor. That became my new normal.

Shame Produces Tired Survivors

A lot of people get stuck as tired survivors. I suppose the reason is because they are surviving and it's difficult to let yourself dream of a better life, or even set goals to attain it. Shame eventually results in a thick shell around your heart. This makes it hard to be in touch with your own heart, and most certainly not allowing others to be close, which makes intimacy almost impossible. In this state you have a massive desire to find escape. You are never satisfied, you feel constant lack, and addictions don't fill the void but simply mask the pain. It's almost as if you become a "fake" person. Your heart isn't open because the overwhelming thought deep down is, "If anyone really knew me, they would reject me."

It becomes obvious when someone lives in shame in that feelings of worthlessness are easily detected. If you feel worthless, it will be virtually impossible to receive anything. This relates to little things or big things, it doesn't matter. You find it hard to receive love, gratitude, or even simple compliments. Because you don't feel you deserve it, your heart refuses to take it, or receive it.

A friend of mine from years ago recently contacted me. She lives in Texas and needed a favor helping her get an item on eBay. My location worked out perfectly in order to assist her in buying a dream collector's item that she always wanted. I was so thankful to have a simple solution for her, and celebrated with her that she found what she had been looking for!

As the conversation continued, she began apologizing for how frivolous this must sound to me. She mentioned that she would like me to keep it a secret because her friends would never understand how this was actually important to her and judge her for the extent of trouble she went through to get it.

"Are you kidding me, Lori?" I said. "Of course I can keep this quiet, but I am celebrating! God knows the desires of your heart. He loves you and is delighted to help you find something that warms you and makes you smile. Don't feel guilty – you have found a treasure and it's only costing you $50!"

What troubles me is that we condemn ourselves too much. We are embarrassed when we pursue a dream in our heart; we feel selfish when we buy ourselves a gift. Let me tell you what God longs for Lori to know: *She is worth it!* God is overjoyed in the moments He can touch our heart – whether that means finding a treasure, or experiencing unexpected pleasures.

When we judge and condemn ourselves, it confirms that we are wearing a cloak of shame. We find ourselves apologizing needlessly and not feeling worthy of love in relationships. Because I know Lori quite intimately, I know that she carries an ongoing secret of an eating disorder. She is defining her life by her failure. That very cloak of a shame is a magnet to judgment.

When we judge and condemn ourselves, it confirms that we are wearing a cloak of shame.

The fantastic news is that Lori doesn't have to continue her life living sub-standard and stay paralyzed in her past. As she begins receiving the unconditional love of God and forgiving and accepting herself as God already has, the cloak of shame will fall off. She will wear a beautiful royal robe of righteousness, that is, she will see herself the way God sees her. Instead of attracting judgment, she will be begin loving herself, then naturally loving those around her with a pure love.

Next time she won't have to apologize! When you start loving yourself, you are able to let yourself indulge in things that make you smile inside. You can laugh easier and enjoy life.

Obviously, *things* can never be your source of life, but you can let them contribute to your happiness without judging yourself for being self-centered and materialistic. God takes pleasure in your prosperity.

The solution to shame is to remind yourself who you are. I am not "once an adulterer always an adulterer.. I am free because of what Jesus did for me. I remind myself that I am righteous in Jesus. I don't have to live with shame as payment for my wrong. I am made new and live a life of peace and godliness. You can too!

about you

- What guilt are your presently ignoring?

- Consider if any of this guilt is misplaced guilt that others are putting on you.

- Is there shame in your heart? How does it make you feel?

meditation

- Take some moments to remind your heart of the truth – that you are valuable and important, and not defined by your mistakes.

- The Bible says that Jesus disregarded or despised the shame.[39] Declare "Shame off me!"

7. REMOVE AVOIDANCE – GO THROUGH THE PAIN

Do you remember doing math problems in school where the teacher asked you to show your work? I especially remember this starting in third grade while learning long division. The teacher wanted to see the process that your mind journeyed in order to find the answer. If you made a mistake, it was much easier to see where you went wrong. This also prevented cheating and using a calculator! The teacher wanted not just the correct answer, but also the understanding of the solution.

You don't need quick-get-fixed answers from God; you need actual solutions by working through life and establishing His truth on your heart. Avoiding pain prevents you from understanding the solutions God has for you. Inviting Him to walk you through pain and learning His character and nature in the process promises reward, authority, and strong character.

My father recently chose to have elective surgery correcting a problem on his eye. The doctors warned him that that there would be three weeks of severe pain during recovery. He counted the cost and decided that it would be more beneficial to endure those three weeks of hardship in expectation of a higher quality of life. Some circumstances force us to choose a season of pain for the greater good.

A couple of years ago I developed pain in my shoulder and I became less and less flexible with each day. I didn't tell anyone of my pain in hopes that it would eventually heal itself. Unfortunately, ignoring the pain didn't help, as it kept getting worse. I told my mom about it and she said that it sounded exactly like the "frozen shoulder" she suffered with when she was about my age.

A friend of ours is an excellent physiotherapist and I found out that a session with him costs $75. I could think of a hundred other things I would rather do with that amount of money so I opted to try and take care of this myself. I kept putting ice on my shoulder and hoped and prayed for the best. A short while later I was at the stove frying up some fajita fixings for Bob and Robert's dinner. A small piece of onion flew over to the other burner. Without much thought, I went to pick it up. For some reason, that burner was also hot, so I jerked my arm back into the air to save my finger from burning. The split-second reaction made my shoulder feel like it had actually left its socket and shooting pain ran through my back, shoulder, and arm.

If only I would have just burned my finger! I started screaming at the top of my lungs, "Help me! Help me! Help me Jesus!" Poor Robert (aged 7 at the time) was horrified since he'd never seen me freak out like that. In between screams I reassured him that I was not going to die, but my arm was killing me. Seriously!

We jumped in the van and drove to our friend's house, the physiotherapist. He put his expertise to work and began checking my shoulder and evaluating the situation. He warned me that the work he was about to do with my deep tissues would be very painful. I chose the pain gladly and said, "Just do what you have to do." I withstood the pain and even paid good money for it. I went back for more torture a couple of times a week for several weeks and paid him – with a smile, a hug, and a huge thank you.

Dealing with pain cost me money and time. So why did I choose to endure more pain? Ignoring and dismissing the pain didn't make it go away. I knew that a season of even greater pain would result in a higher quality of life, and it's worth it!

In order for there to be transformation in your life, you may have to face realities that you were hoping would just go away. You may have to make tough decisions that will result in pain because you are hoping for a higher quality of life. Living life craving instant gratification will cost you dearly in the long run and does not have the substance to take you the distance.

You may have to make tough decisions that will result in pain because you are hoping for a higher quality of life.

Persevere *Through*

Getting to the place of liking yourself means you uncover the secrets that you are carrying and persevere *through*. I like the saying credited to Winston Churchill, "If you're going through hell, keep going." The last thing to do when you are in a hard place is to stop. Keep going and get the help you need!

Ali introduced herself to me as a single mom who had an affair with her best friend's husband and hasn't been able to live with herself. The secret was intact, but she couldn't carry the guilt another day. The torment involved in the consequences for her sin had been painful and disabling. She hated herself for what she did.

I didn't have all the answers for her, but I did know the first step. I encouraged Ali to find her place of peace. By telling me about the affair, she broke the power of the secret she had been carrying. However, she was in hyper-confusion and chaos, and that's never a good time to make a life-altering decision. In order to deal with the massive amount of confusion in Ali's heart and find peace, I asked her some pointed questions to find her anchor of what she believed: *What do you know to be true? Do you believe God is real? Do you believe He loves you? Have you asked Him to forgive you?*

Her answers were yes, yes and yes. I said, "Since you have asked God to forgive you, then you are forgiven completely and totally. Your forgiveness and cleansing is not in question. The guilt you feel from what you did has motivated you to 'come clean' with God. He has not left you and He wants to walk with you as you live through the difficult consequences in the days to come. Because of the peace and love of God, even though there are many unknowns about the future, you can function, you can take care of your kids, and you will have to be intentional about what you think about. Meditating on God's love and grace will enable you to continue. Every day, worship God and thank Him for His forgiveness and mercy."

After establishing the peace of God and relationship with Him, Ali faced difficult decisions. The reason she still felt guilty is because she was living a lie in her relationship with her best friend. She didn't want the affair to destroy her friend's family and wanted her marriage to be saved. Unfortunately, there was no guarantee that this would be the outcome.

Should she tell her friend what she did? There are no cut and dry answers when it comes to revealing this type of information. Some marriages will not survive the crisis of an affair. Bob and I have experienced and believe that any marriage can be saved when both individuals are willing to walk the journey of restoration. Ali decided to talk to the husband first and give him 24 hours to tell his wife about the betrayal. If he didn't tell her, Ali would. The husband refused, as he wanted to keep it a secret, so Ali told her friend. She decided this is the most loving thing she could do. She took full ownership of her betrayal and withstood the painful repercussions. Her hope and prayer is that the family will stay together, and she is extremely remorseful for participating in selfish behavior that quite possibly could end a marriage.

In the next season of her life, Ali knows there are painful days ahead, but she is full of hope for her future. She knows that she will have to deal with shame that has most likely been the soil in the garden of her heart. There will be challenges. There are irreversible consequences. The woman who was once her best friend might possibly be angry with her forever. Others will discover what happened and she may face public ridicule. But she's not alone. In her pain, she has run into the arms of Jesus who is walking with her every day and not defining her by her past. There was no way to be evacuated out of her situations, but God is walking her *through*.

Countless times, I have been asked the question from women who have had affairs whether they absolutely have to tell their husbands about the infidelity. Because I believe this is a personal decision, I tremble to be dogmatic or insist that they confess. However, from my experience I have a belief written on my heart: *The truth shall set you free.*[40]

When I confessed my adultery to Bob, I had full realization that I was entering a season of extreme pain and soon discovered it was even worse than I thought it would be. But would I have done things differently? Absolutely not. The quality of life and relationship that we have as a result of radical transparency and restoration is something I deeply treasure and it was developed through times of pain together.

The End of Yourself Starts it All

I just got off the phone with a guy – a youth pastor from Maryland, twenty-eight years old, married for six years. He heard our marriage story a few years ago and has now found himself in a desperate place. His wife had a sexual affair. Now they are separated, he's confused and doesn't know how to forgive her.

From the few minutes I spent listening to him, I could conclude that he was an angry person, but was desperate for answers. Through tears, he confessed his responsibility in the marriage breakdown, that he had hit his wife and abused her verbally. What do we tell someone who is in this magnitude of pain and regret?

I could hear his heart of sorrow through his words. There is something very beautiful about a person who is in a place of humility and desiring to change – no matter what it takes. We could have spent an hour talking about the reasons she had the affair and hash out a game plan for getting her back and restoring the marriage. However, that's not what this guy needed. At least not yet. He needed to find the love of his heavenly Father before anything else.

Every angry person is desperate for love. Not just any love, but the extravagant, unconditional, relentless, over-the-top, not-holding-your-mistakes-against-you love that only our Father in heaven can give us. I told him that before he pursues the marriage, he must receive God's love for him and let Him heal his broken heart.

Instead of seeing himself at the bottom with no where to go, I encouraged him to see this place of pain and desperation as the *perfect place for God to reach him* in places of his heart that he has never been willing to go before. Because he had abused his wife, I assumed that he had been abused as well. So I told him that there were places in his heart that were so painful and dark, he had never visited them. He began to sob. This was his opportunity to embrace the pain, take courage, and bring God with him. I said, "This is about you as a little boy – hurting, broken, and abused where lies were written on your heart: *Unlovable. Not worthy to be loved. Rejected.* Today, run into the arms of your heavenly Daddy and let him hold you and cry together. God never wanted those things to happen to you. They never should have happened."

God wants to write truth on his heart, the truth that he is loved unconditionally. God is not disappointed in him. He can stop trying so hard. He can fall into God's arms and find rest and peace.

As this guy embarks on the journey of being loved and receiving love, everything – and I mean everything – in his life will change. He won't have to try hard to forgive his wife because when he forgives himself, he will effortlessly give his wife that same gift. He won't have to try so hard to stop being angry, because when you know you're loved, the anger literally dissipates. It's not about anger-management; it's about God's finished work in his heart. If anger or unforgiveness tries to creep back in, he will simply need to remind his heart of the truth – *I am fully and completely loved.*

He quietly started weeping and said, "I have preached sermons about the love of the Father, but nobody has ever reached me here and I've never understood it like this before…"

I reminded him, "You are in a desperate place of pain, but you are willing to walk to places you have avoided your whole life. This painful place is the most significant opportunity you have ever had to experience a completely transformed life."

The reason I have authority to speak to this young man and effectively communicate the love of God to him is because I've lived through pain. I would have loved to avoid the pain of facing my sinful and selfish choice to have an affair and pretend it didn't happen. But circumstances forced me to courageously forge ahead. At the time it would have been so much easier to have an abortion, but now, ten years later, I enjoy God's reward.

I could not be more thankful that Jesus walked me *through* the valley of the shadow of death.[41]

What pain are you experiencing? Instead of ignoring it and hoping it will go away, are you ready to face the consequences and embrace the pain knowing that there is a promise of freedom on the other side? Facing the truth can be very overwhelming. There are many times I just wanted to quit and run. Maybe you've felt like that too. The truth is that Jesus is pursuing you. He is your friend and involving Him in this painful season of your journey is absolutely crucial. Jesus sees the tears you cry at night and He holds you as you pray. You are not alone, and your current pain has the potential to launch you forward as you press on.

about you

- Recall a painful season in your life where you trusted God and found new levels of understanding and peace that you may not have received any other way.

- Are you in a present season of pain? What does going *through* look like for you?

- What do you believe to be God's wisdom, comfort, perspective, and solution right now?

meditation

I believe this is a moment of time in your life when you are closing a chapter and starting a new one. As you turn the page, you are determined to remove everything that's hindering full-on happiness and you will discover that you were born with a purpose at just the right time. God wrote this letter to His people many years ago. Read it as if He is saying it to you today:

Dear Zion,

Don't despair.

Your God is present among you,

A strong Warrior there to save you.

Happy to have you back, he'll calm you with his love and delight you with his songs.[42]

chapter 9

fulfilling responsibility
...without sacrificing the fun

*You can have it all – the joy of fulfilling
responsibility plus freedom to belly laugh and rise
above the circumstances. When you're having fun,
you are better at what you do and your zeal for life
is contagious!*

I've seen it too many times. Women doing everything they're expected to do, but sacrificing the fun-factor and hating their lives. Who says you can't like yourself, love your life, and still be responsible? When it comes to responsibility and fun, people presume we have to choose one or the other. Some think that if you're going to be conscientious and dependable, then doing the right thing means sacrificing the fun, at least most of the time. Let's explore this from a new vantage point. What if responsibility and fun can work hand in hand like perfect partners fueling each other toward efficiency, greatness, and enjoying each moment? We presume happiness is a luxury, but we were created to live and work with joy in our hearts. Anything less is substandard existence.

Our warped view of responsibility has created an invisible contest within us where we subconsciously believe that if we are responsible enough, we can reward ourselves with enjoyment and rest. The person being driven to be responsible without interjecting spontaneity and fun observes the "irresponsible" one who throws caution to the wind and and screams, "You need to take life more seriously! I'm being loyal to my husband and kids, my dead-end job, paying my bills, living a stable existence, and this other one flies by the seat of her pants, loves life, neglects responsibility and things go well for her! It doesn't make sense! I thought diligence, loyalty, and integrity comes with a reward!" They don't believe they can be responsible and still have fun.

Your strong will and self-control that is helping you make responsible choices does come with reward, but if you are living a lifeless, "do-the-right-thing" existence, you are missing the fire that wants to be stoked within you. The deception of fulfilling everyone's expectations, including your own quickly leads to a life of disappointment. It doesn't take long until your daily tasks become mundane and you are busy and bored at the same time.

The other extreme is the girl with a selfish and lazy attitude who just wants to have fun, fun, and more fun without contributing to the ones who need her. Ignoring our responsibilities will not make them go away. As princess-warrior girls we want to live a life worthy of our calling...live our life without limits and run the race to win. The key is to embrace our responsibility without ignoring our longing for pleasure and fun. What makes you a winner are not just your accomplishments, but also your joy in the journey.

I have the pleasure of meeting new friends when I travel and speak in various cities. I love sharing funny stories. It seems to break down walls of being guarded, and before long, women are telling me some hilarious life experiences of their own. Inevitably, I will meet a woman and our conversation will become animated, witty, and downright silly as we tell stories of shocking situations including embarrassing mama moments and farting accidentally in public. Okay, having gas. Sorry if that offended anyone.

After belly laughing for several minutes the moment suddenly becomes sober. It's as if the girl I'm with will catch herself and look at me with deep longing in her eyes and say, "I don't laugh like this anymore. I take myself too seriously. It's been too long. This belly-laughing is feeling really good." Everything in me wants to dig deep into her soul and find that child-like girl who loves dancing, twirling, and smiling for no apparent reason. I want her to be free to love unguardedly, break through the shell of disappointment, and start living real life again.

Do you find yourself going to jobs because you have to, cleaning because you have to, parenting because you have to, making love because you have to, waking up because you have to? What happened to doing things because you *want* to? This very heart condition can lead to a desperate state where you do shocking things. You believe you would be better off with a new husband, or a new city, and begin looking for answers in all the wrong places. No matter where you go, there you are. The problem will not be solved by changing the outward circumstances, but rather through finding happiness and fulfillment inside of you. If you are relating to this, don't lose heart. It's never too late to break away from the life you hate, and you can do it without walking away from your relationships and responsibilities.

It's never too late to break away from the life you hate, and you can do it without walking away from your relationships and responsibilities.

The difference between surviving and thriving often hinges on this very paradigm. If you are being responsible and doing the right thing, there is a strong chance that you are surviving. You are paying your bills, you are managing to stay in your relationships, and you are doing the best you can as mom to your kids.

Fast-forward now to the girl who has forgiven herself, accepted her past, and is free from the fear of the future. You'll meet a girl who laughs easy, knows God's comfort, and is smiling in the security of knowing she's completely loved. That's thriving. That's the one who not only pays her bills, but also knows God as her Provider and the One who takes pleasure in her prosperity. Not only does she have peace in her relationships, but also enjoys the passion, vibrancy, and joy that comes with loving people. Not only is she a mom, but her children also adore her and don't feel judged by her. That's being responsible *and* fun.

In most things, if you are enjoying something you are going to be better at it. Think of your job, your responsibility as a mother, and of everything that's required of you. If you can fulfill that duty and decide to love it, you will begin to thrive in that very thing! I can't help but think of our little guy's school bus driver. His name is Cowboy Bob and he enjoys his job.

Every weekday morning we exchange smiles, greetings, and poke a little fun, and it ends with him pointing at all of us parents saying, "Keep your powder dry!" I'm guessing that has something to do with cowboy-gun-language, but whatever it is, you better believe I remember to *always* keep my powder dry and I appreciate him loving his job, because it makes him really good at it. He's being responsible and loving life all at the same time.

What areas of life are you responsible for effortlessly? Even though there's hard work involved, you never question the sacrifice? That's because "your heart is in it." Enjoying what you do isn't *only* about modifying your behavior and trying to be your own cheerleader. Those things are all good, but true and lasting transformation starts with your heart, identifying the lies you have believed that limit you from forgiving yourself. Loving life effortlessly requires us to do "heart work" and be willing to face our disempowering beliefs.

This last year we have featured Dr. Jim Richards on our daily program, *It's A New Day* every Thursday morning. He teaches extensively about *Heart Physics*, which is dealing with our hearts. This email response to the show just came in last week:

> I have been watching Dr. Jim Richards on your program and can't wait to tell you what happened to me. When I was twenty-one, I was single and arrived home from the hospital with a new baby out of wedlock. I was getting ready to go out on a Saturday night and my mom looked at me and said, "Where are you going? Don't you know that you have a responsibility now?" From that moment in my life it felt like I was in a football stadium and the lights got shut off as I stumbled through life. I am now fifty years old and was never able to have fun. I always had to be responsible. After searching my heart for the first time with the help of Jim Richard's teaching, I am able to see clearly that the words my mom said were not to tell me I wasn't *good*, she was simply reminding me that even though I was young, I needed to step up. As of today, I believe the truth. I have forgiven myself. I no longer have to prove myself by being extra-responsible. I am loved and accepted. I feel like years of disappointment, pain, and even my tough exterior have washed off. This happened yesterday and for the first time in over 29 years I feel like I am on cloud nine.... I have believed a lie and even though fulfilling responsibility helped me start my own business and buy and sell over thirty-five homes, it never allowed me to have a life. I cannot

say thank you enough for making a way for me to understand for the first time. I feel free!

I have always craved freedom and fun. I used to apologize for it. Now I understand that this isn't a selfish desire, but rather a God-given provision to keep my life thriving, contagious, and passionate. Psalms 18:19 says:

> [God] brought me out into a *spacious* place; he rescued me because he delighted in me.[43]

It's easy to dance, run free, and enjoy limitless pleasure when you are in a spacious place. Just imagine what little kids are like when you let them out of a small room and put them on a playground! The most important part of a spacious place that usually gets unnoticed is that there are boundaries and fences that keep the spacious place a safe place.

It's easy to dance, run free, and enjoy limitless pleasure when you are in a spacious place.

It's the same with me. I can enjoy dancing and freedom because there are personal boundaries established in my heart that cannot be moved. These are beliefs in my heart that keep me safe. I can enjoy life because I also enjoy my responsibilities, know that moral compromise will always lead to pain, and refuse to believe it will bring me lasting pleasure.

REWARDS OF RESPONSIBILITY

Hard work and fulfilling our responsibilities can lead to success, wealth, and a long life.[44] I used to envy those who appeared to have it all and just thought they were lucky. They were the ones who got that big break that everyone wants. But if you study the lives of those who are living their dreams and influencing others, most have been diligent and responsible and have refused to give up when the going got tough. Responsibility is full of rewards.

Reward: Confirmation of Self-Worth and Confidence

There is a connection between responsibility and the personal value we feel. Being responsible leads to accomplishing. Accomplishing great or small tasks feeds our confidence. Personal confidence feeds our worth, and our worth feeds our confidence.

After years of working with individuals and couples regarding relationship issues, we can see how every person needs to fight through memories of rejection and need for approval and simply receive the worth that God has for them. If you know your value, you are more able to conquer obstacles of rejection and introspection. If you know your value, you are able to receive unconditional love and then channel it out towards others. When you have victory over worthlessness, life truly becomes what it was meant to be.

Being responsible does not necessarily lead to greater revelation of your worth in God. However, once I have received revelation of the worth that I have in God and am convinced that I no longer have to *work* to be approved, I find myself tackling new responsibilities! Resting in my worth and approval doesn't mean I don't have to do anything anymore. I don't sit at home on my couch, cuddle my dog, bask in this worth and do nothing! (Well, sometimes I do…sigh!) But mostly I it motivates me to be responsible for what God has given me to do.

Growing in *self-worth* is a journey that includes a parallel passage of growing in *self-confidence*. It's like using both feet to walk. When you know your *worth* (left foot), you are able to tackle a responsibility and fulfill a passion that you could not have done otherwise. You leave your comfort zone and forge ahead into what was previously not possible. The result of succeeding at something you have never done before and breaking free from limitations gives you *self-confidence* (right foot). That

Growing in self-worth is a journey that includes a parallel passage of growing in self-confidence.

newfound *self-confidence* then leads you to take another step deeper in *self-worth* (left foot). Then again, you achieve success in taking another action, building your *self-confidence* (right foot). This journey allows you to live your fullest life and yet have the ability to rest and have fun.

Having true self-worth will always involve action that supports the beliefs or the way you view yourself. Feeling good about yourself without taking appropriate action will not strengthen your confidence. It will actually weaken it. The Bible makes an important connection between our faith (who we are and what we believe) and what we do:

> What good is it, dear brothers and sisters, if you say you have faith but don't show it by your actions? … faith is dead without good works.[45]

In the same way that our faith dies unless there are corresponding actions, our self-worth only grows as we are responsible for the tasks God gives to us so that we can become all that He has created us to be. Our worth grows and is established as we reach out to fulfill passion, and develop confidence in taking responsibility for what we value. One of the rewards of fulfilling responsibility is that it confirms our worth. And knowing your worth establishes your confidence in life.

Reward: Experiencing Fulfillment

I wouldn't have guessed that I love responsibility, but my value system says I do. The telltale gauge for knowing what you value is simply observing what you make sacrifices for. You will sacrifice for the thing you value. I will sacrifice to get my work done, have a beautiful clean home, and have order in our finances and life. The hard work is worth it, but even better, we can find joy *within* our work!

Fulfilling responsibility can actually be...fulfilling. In a very practical way, getting things done brings satisfaction. Let's close our eyes and imagine a few feel-good moments.

The laundry is done...it's warm, it smells fresh, and it's put away. The laundry baskets are empty. The drawers are full. Ahhhh... life is good.

The dishes are clean and put away. The kitchen is shiny and wiped clean and that patio door window is free from handprints and doggie-nose wetness. Ahhhh...life is good.

The little guy is asleep in his bed. His tummy is full. There is peace in this moment and his face looks like an angel. (Why, oh why, do kids manage to look like angels when they're asleep?) Ahhhh...life is good.

You've worked hard all week and you sit down to pay the bills and there's enough money in your account. Ahhhh...what a relief!

The family is together and something funny happens and there are barrels of laughter ringing through the house. Ahhhh...life is good.

You have responsibilities that only you know, and your feel-good moments are most likely different than mine. But instead of hating your responsibilities and running from them, remember the rewards they offer and face procrastination and fear of failure head on. As you learn to like yourself, remember your intentional self-talk. Tell yourself how much you appreciate your hard work. Congratulate yourself and remember that you are never alone. God wants you to experience His benefits every single day and give you the wisdom to accomplish your very purpose for living.

When we're out of town, our daughter Janelle (21) has huge responsibilities. In addition to her fulltime job, she takes full responsibility for Robert and the home including groceries, homework, cooking, cleaning, and juggling schedules. She recently told me how she invented a game that she plays with herself. When she feels unmotivated and exhausted and the house is a mess and the dishes are dirty, she sets the timer on the stove for twenty minutes and decides to go crazy cleaning until the time is up. After that, she rewards herself with rest and relaxation. She is amazed every time at the amount of things she can get done when she's in power-mode! Sometimes we waste 20 minutes just trying to psyche ourselves up, and then end up wasting time thinking about stuff instead of just getting it done.

WHAT SHOULD YOU BE RESPONSIBLE FOR?

Responsibility without enjoyment dies a slow death, but the fact is, responsibility isn't always fun. We all have to do stuff we don't feel like doing. In fact, we do a lot of things we wouldn't choose to do if we actually had the choice. And many of us are carrying more than we can bear. We are simply overloaded with responsibility. Please, please recognize when you have too many responsibilities for a human being to fulfill. We do have limits! Most of us are running on empty, our adrenals are shot, and we are about to crash and burn. With so many responsibilities out there each begging for your attention, you have to be very deliberate about what you take responsibility for and what you need to let go of each day. Let's look at our main responsibilities.

Be Responsible to Keep First What You Value Most

Take an account of what you need to sacrifice before it's too late. If you are intentional and take your responsibilities into account, there are things you can stop doing. You will sacrifice for what you value most. So does it match up? I've asked myself this and it didn't add up at all. Not too long ago I evaluated where I was spending the most time – speaking and traveling. Sure, it was furthering my career and my sphere of influence, but in the middle of my mission of "fighting for families" was I sacrificing my very own?

I'm using my own life as an example, but you can apply this to yours as well. I have to ask myself some very tough questions:

- Am I too busy traveling and speaking because I am seeking some sort of approval from people?
- Am I doing it for added income? Has my lifestyle crept up to a level that is challenging to maintain?
- Are there changes I can implement that will enable me to continue influencing people while maintaining more time at home?

I found myself with very little time at home. In your particular line of work, do you find yourself in the same predicament? Where is there lack in your life? Where are you overwhelmed with responsibility? I spoke about this in New Zealand a couple of months ago and a single mom spoke to me afterwards. A light had turned on for her as she forced herself to work sixty hours a week in order for her children to have everything they needed and wanted to fit a secure lifestyle. She admitted, "Just before attending this women's conference, my little seven-year-old had tears in her eyes asking me why I have to work all the time. I just presumed I had to. Now I'm not so sure. My kids want me home more than they want every latest toy and fancy gadget."

The very reason you are overwhelmed with responsibility could possibly be altered as you make lifestyle changes. Are you trying to please people and gain approval? If you have any fear of rejection or are in need of approval, it's likely that you are trying too hard to be the answer for your friends and people may be taking advantage of you. Or you may be attempting to achieve an impressive exterior by meeting the status quo in where you live, how you look, and who your friends are.

Take a hard look at what you are sacrificing. Then look at what you think you value most. If they don't match up, be willing to take a hard look at your life and make needed changes to what you've taken on as responsibilities. It's not easy to say "no" where you are needed and wanted, and I personally hate disappointing anyone. But you will never please all of the people all of the time anyway! If you're not laughing easily in life, there's a good chance that you are due to make some changes.

My traditional thinking forces me to place my priorities on a measuring stick and put one ahead of the other. You may have grown up with this acronym: **J**esus, **O**thers, **Y**ourself = JOY! This is a wonderful outlook in living unselfishly, but it trains us to put our priorities in a pecking order instead of seeing our life as a circle with God in the center as our Source for everything, and then everything else branching out from that circle.

We don't have to force ourselves to decide that one is more important than the other, for God wants you to put value on your husband, your children, fulfilling purpose through work and ministry, friends, your health, and your finances. I don't have to sacrifice my children in order to have a great marriage. I don't have to sacrifice my health in order to have enough money.

I can place value on *all* of these areas of my life knowing God as my Source, knowing that He will give me wisdom moment-by-moment as to where I should give my time, attention, and energy.

Be Responsible to be Realistic

As much as I crave rest and enjoyment, I find it challenging to stop and take a break when there is so much to do. I take my responsibilities very seriously. How can I sit around when there are things to be done? There are lists to be crossed out! Plans to fulfill! Goals to accomplish!

Jesus only did what he saw his Father doing.[46] He had a whole world to save, and yet he knew when to stop. The story of Mary and Martha in the Bible is a great reminder to set our compass on "being" rather than "doing."[47] Martha was busy with her lists and Mary sat at the feet of Jesus gazing into his face and hanging on his every word. Sometimes I can relate to Martha and feel her frustration. There are things that must be done, responsibilities that must be fulfilled, so how can she just sit there? Then other times I can easily relate to Mary. I can't help but wonder who was serving Jesus the best, for if Jesus wanted a glass of water, who would be the first one he would ask? I think it would have been Mary. She was right there, ready to serve him in whatever he needed. Could it be that Martha had unrealistic expectations on herself and as a result couldn't serve Jesus effectively?

We also need to identify unrealistic expectations. If you have unrealistically high expectations of yourself, it's likely that you inflict those on others around you! What you deem important, you naturally assume others should too. Martha believed that her responsibilities were most important. The pressure she put on herself turned into criticism of the one she loved. What you believe makes you responsible is the measuring stick you use to evaluate others. The problem is that everyone has a very separate and unique measuring stick when it comes to what's important and what makes a person responsible!

What you believe makes you responsible is the measuring stick you use to evaluate others.

One lady confided in me the things that bugged her about her husband. Among the nit-picky things was that he didn't take time to watch the news, but chose irrelevant and shallow entertainment for his TV viewing. She felt that it was important to keep current and be informed. Our conversation lightened as I confessed that I was exactly like her husband. Yet I told her how grateful I am that Bob is interested and keeps up on the news so that I can excuse myself from what I find repetitive and negative.

We all have unique convictions in what makes us responsible. Be true to yourself. It sounds cliché, but God made you for a purpose, so putting undue expectations on yourself will distract you from having the time and energy to be who you are.

We take on responsibilities we were never meant to carry. Get yourself in a quiet place and ask God to speak to your heart to begin the process of identifying the tasks and relationships that have become excess baggage. Responsibility is a partnership with God. You are on this earth for a purpose, and God wants your life to be full of His benefits.[48] He wants to give you wisdom and insight into what you should be spending your time doing, and then He wants to do those things with you. Let me say it another way: *God wants you to know exactly what you should be responsible for in the moment, and then He wants to work with you as you fulfill those responsibilities.* It brings me tremendous comfort to know that I am never alone no matter what I'm doing or where I am.

Be Responsible for Your Thoughts

I was recently watching a Disney movie and the villain was plotting to annihilate the princess and dissipate the royal lineage. Every evil plan he attempted would end with defeat as the princess slipped away from danger and death just in the knick of time. Tormented by failure, he had to dream up a more devious plan in order to destroy her once and for all. In his wildly vicious tone he finally said, "That's it! I'll get into her mind. She can't escape me there! Mwa-hahahah!"[49]

I don't know about you, but I can be in my car and drive from point A to point B and entertain any thought that jumped into my head. But if you asked me what I thought about, I would have to really think about it! This tells me that I am just letting myself think by default, meaning whatever thoughts want to fleet in and out of my mind, whether good, bad, angry, accusing, happy or sad, my mind lets them in and follow their course. Unfortunately, that's how the enemy gets in to annihilate the princess – you! "That's it! I'll get into her mind. She can't escape me there!"

Thankfully the Bible offers us a clear directive on how we are to think and it has served me well in directing my life.

> And now, dear brothers and sisters, one final thing. Fix your thoughts on what is true, and honorable, and right, and pure, and lovely, and admirable. Think about things that are excellent and worthy of praise. Keep putting into practice all you learned and received from me—everything you heard from me and saw me doing. Then the God of peace will be with you.[50]

God's word doesn't give any room for negativity. So, is it possible to edit our thoughts and truly diminish negative thinking? Can we actually be free from downward spirals of thinking that we're failures, we're not good enough, we're rejected, we're alone, we're in lack, and we are ultimately unlovable? Can we refuse to judge others when we've been unfairly judged? I say, "Yes!" When you catch yourself thinking negatively, realize that the thought has already developed an emotion and it's building up the steam the more you meditate on it to send you into action! In this moment, not only do you need to bite your lip, but take notice and later identify the lie that you believe in your heart.

Directing your thoughts means you are directing your life. What you habitually think about is prophesying your future.

Directing your thoughts means you are directing your life. What you habitually think about is prophesying your future. On the other hand, letting your thoughts run wild each day will result in a life lived by default. Editing your thoughts takes effort – sometimes a lot of effort – but the reward is a life full of peace and joy.[51]

Renewing the mind brings peace of mind

You are thinking and even meditating all day long. You have formed habits of what you allow yourself to think about. You've probably heard the expression, "One thought leads to another." It's actually true that you think in patterns, and when you return to a pattern of thought repeatedly, it will ultimately determine your life's direction. Renewing your mind will be a challenge, much like breaking a bad habit. There is a process of resisting negative cycles of thinking and forging new neurological paths through your brain.

Consider how long you've allowed fearful and unloving thoughts to permeate your mind – but that can change! A precious girl called me in desperation as she struggled with suspicion against her husband. Even though her fears weren't validated, she just couldn't seem to trust him and spent her days like a detective, trying to find evidence to use against him. Her husband couldn't do anything to convince her that he wasn't a lust-driven pervert. This unprecedented jealousy was driving her (and him!) crazy. This obsession stole her joy and was bringing a strain to her marriage. Her imagination was being used to imagine that her husband was betraying her.

At the end of her rope, she was ready to try anything. Pain and desperation is a tremendous opportunity to identify lies on our hearts and replace them with truth. I love what she did next.

In humility, she chose to stop blaming him for her problem and took a brave look at her own fears and dysfunction. She got alone with God, quieted her thoughts, and asked God to help her identify the reason she didn't feel safe and protected, and why her fear of rejection and betrayal was ruling her life. God lovingly reminded her of incidents that took place in her past, things she was scared to think about, mostly because it made them real and she wanted to wish them away. In her efforts to ignore them or stuff them, the hurt begged to be noticed and revealed itself in anger, judgment, and bitterness.

Bringing God into those memories, incidents, and hurtful words that were spoken, she allowed herself to grieve and mourn, all the while imagining herself in her heavenly Father's arms, the safest place to be. In the days following, she intentionally persuaded her heart of the truth.

Resisting the thoughts that had now become normal and habitual for twenty years, she fought through the patterns of thinking and recited her newfound truth: "I have nothing to fear. God's perfect love expels fear. My Father in heaven will protect me and heal my broken heart. He will never leave me. I can trust Him."

Thinking these new thoughts is extremely challenging. You have to be determined, courageous, and desperate enough to leave the familiar and forge new territory. Because our thinking forms neurological pathways in our brain, thinking the same way with the same thoughts for twenty years turns pathways into well-paved freeways! And if you think by default, you will automatically choose the easiest and most familiar thoughts.

To think new thoughts, I imagine myself as an explorer in a rainforest with a huge machete in my hand. Even though it would be easier to get on that freeway, it is not benefiting my life. Instead, I will start the process of making a new path. No matter how much effort it takes to gain new ground, I will persevere until I get through.

It is worth every ounce of effort you put into this. This precious girl has experienced heart transformation. It has been two years since she stopped blaming others and pursued healing for her own heart. As God has calmed her fears, her new thought patterns that were once like a rainforest are now well-paved freeways, and living in peace has become effortless.

Every time you are intentional to interrupt a negative thought and redirect your thinking to follow a new pattern, you are renewing your mind. You are setting a new neurological pathway in your brain and it will be easier the next time. In everyday life, there are family dynamics, financial stress, and health issues that can influence your heart to fall into negativity. God wants to help you live a life of victory every single day, and you can change the way you think.

Since understanding this concept, when I catch myself thinking self-degrading thoughts, I interrupt that pattern of thought. The best way to make permanent change in this area and change what was once normal is to shock yourself when you find yourself thinking in the old pattern. Consider doing something drastic in order to shock your system! As soon as you catch yourself thinking thoughts of fear, or beating yourself up, grab a glass of cold water and splash it in your face!

Wear a rubber band around your wrist and snap it! Burst into a song! Pinch your nipples! Do something that works for you, but make a decision to refuse negative thinking. And don't just refuse negative thinking, speak out positive thoughts about yourself. Be your own best friend – and best encourager – like we talked about earlier in this book.

As we begin to think differently, we will live differently. These new thinking patterns will give you the authority to overcome addictions. Just like this girl who was addicted to thinking jealous thoughts and gave into the fear that paralyzed her life, maybe you've been labeled as one who is prone to addiction problems. That is a lie that has been written on your heart and you don't have to believe it for another day! God has the power to impart truth to your heart that enables you to be assured, beyond a shadow of a doubt, that God is your Source of comfort, your Refuge when you feel like escaping, your Unconditional Love when you feel unlovable. He is everything you need.

Be Responsible to Keep a Thankful Heart

Everyone can choose to be grateful. Your entire point of view can shift the second you think about what you're thankful for, even in the middle of trying to fulfill so many responsibilities. Thankfulness leads to hope, and when you have hope, you are unstoppable.

When I was eighteen in college in Texas, there was a rumor going around about a southern preacher with a loud voice who had the reputation of starting his sermons with a profound and powerful opening statement. On this one particular evening with a group of two thousand leaders, he walked on stage, took hold of the microphone and intended to say, "Praise God! I've got hope in my soul tonight!" He got the letters a little mixed up when he accidentally said, "Praise God! I've got soap in my hole tonight!" Even though his message didn't come out right, hope in our soul is definitely something to praise God for. And it comes through having a thankful heart.

Winston is our Labradoodle dog. He's humongous, playful, and as happy as a clam. His enthusiasm for life bubbles over and you can't help but smile. The other day our son Robert said, "I love Winston. He's just like a person. A really dumb person." Another fallacy about being happy is that it makes a person appear dumb – one who doesn't take life seriously. I can't help but think of SpongeBob. I'm personally quite inspired by the little yellow square guy. He's happy, sports an insanely positive attitude, and always thinks the best of people. The other day Robert was in the yard doing his least favorite chore, what we like to call "poop-patrol"…did I mention that Winston is a very large dog? Robert was tempted to have a bad attitude, so I told him to think of a happy song. He began singing a song by SpongeBob, "Mr. Sun came out and he smiled at me. He said it's gonna be a good one just wait and see! Jumped out of bed and I ran outside feeling so extra exstatified…it's the best day ever!"[52]

All of a sudden he stopped concentrating on the poop and got lost in his song. What a lesson for me to remember. It can be my life quote: "Stop concentrating on the poop and get lost in the song…" We can live through almost any kind of hardship when we choose joy and sing our way through it. And the key word in that lesson is *through*. Singing *through* a tough season of life doesn't mean we are dumb or in denial. Earlier in this book I described how God brought me *through* my painful circumstances. When we choose to avoid evacuation and face the painful places in our heart that need to be plowed, God grows something beautiful. He gives us beauty for ashes.

I double-dog-dare you to smile during the stuff you don't enjoy. Turn on your favorite music if at all possible! If it's housework you have to do, you can dance and power-clean at the same time. If that isn't enough for you to smile and have fun, then take your clothes off. That only works when you're alone - unless it's your husband. (That'll shock him! And he might really like it!) Oh yeah, and close the blinds and don't answer the door. Just some practical rules for cleaning naked – common sense, really.

I'll even venture to say that the more happy I am and the more I laugh and have fun, the better I do in my role as mom, wife, friend, daughter, sister, worker, and boss. (Just writing all our roles out in one sentence can give us a hint as to why we feel stress! Talk about changing hats a million times a day!) I can't emphasize the power of thankfulness enough. Even when circumstances seem impossible and unfair, you can always be thankful that God is crazy about you, He has not left you alone, and He cares about the details of your life.

Be Responsible to Find Fun

Part of loving myself is getting to know myself. I know what makes me smile, what brings security, and what gives me comfort. I have stopped apologizing for my sometimes-crazy-whacked personality and embraced the truth that God made me in my unique expression of Himself. Fun is very high priority for me and I love to belly laugh. Being alone with God is pretty much my favorite thing in the world, and I thank God for my husband and kids several times a day. Even though I am a people-person, strangely enough I am energized and rejuvenated when I am by myself. I ask God to help me identify lies that are still on my heart and I firmly establish truth in my belief system.

The girl with the happy heart knows herself and loves herself. What about you? Stop for a second and answer these questions:

- What are your favorite things in the world?
- What makes you feel secure?
- What makes you smile?
- How do you get energized?
- What do you love most about yourself?

Was answering these questions easy or difficult? If it was hard, then you have some learning to do about yourself! There's good clean fun in your future, custom designed for your sense of humor, and it's up to you to make it happen. You can't expect fun to find you, even though it's wonderful when it does. The first step to finding fun is to nurture fun-loving relationships – relationships where the chemistry is electric and the enjoyment is effortless. No success in the world can replace the value of friendship and family in relationships you thrive in. If you need more friends, be a good friend, consider other's needs, and be generous in listening. Put yourself out there and join clubs and events, volunteer, and get out of your comfort zone. There are people just like you looking for friends. So find each other!

What is your fun factor? I don't pretend to think that everyone enjoys the same kind of fun as me. There are flavors of fun and you have a favorite. Instead of feeling misunderstood, identifying your unique sense of humor will help you to find people who appreciate you and share your idea of a good time.

Are you witty? This is the smart person who is quick and ready to express illuminating and amusing comments with spontaneity and cleverness. She is a genius and usually keeps a straight face during execution. If you are naturally witty, here's a way to have fun: Find people who enjoy deep conversations, broaden your interests, and develop knowledge about things that interest you most.

Are you silly? Probably the opposite of witty, being silly is laughing at meaningless and mindless behavior. Random and pointless, this kind of humor is characterized by unexpected and shocking stories, double-dog dares, and a lot of belly laughing.

Maybe you love putting yourself at risk, or enjoy the thrill of competition in sports! Bob loves to use his mind and it's fun for him to do a Sudoku puzzle. I wouldn't pick up one of these puzzles if my life depended on it! But he's trying to convince me that it's terrific exercise for the brain.

Helping others is one of the most fulfilling activities on the face of the earth. It's fun to discover a need and find a way to meet it. Some find fun in taking on a project and seeing it through. Others love to relax with a garnished drink. God gave us our senses to enjoy touch and smell and to take in sights and sounds. Music, massages, sports, movies, walks in nature, laying on a hammock, quiet time with God, visiting with friends, bungee jumping, power walking...you are your own definition of a good time. God understands pleasure! That's why he made food to taste good, sex to feel good, and sunsets to look good.

Celebrate the way God made you to love life. Drink in His refreshment and smile easily.

about you

- Make a list of all of your responsibilities – and I mean *all* of them. Mark which ones bring you the greatest satisfaction, and which ones only keep you busy with very little return on investment. Then look at your list. Are you overwhelmed with too much responsibility?

- What responsibilities are you are doing just to look good or prove yourself?

- What are some of the unrealistic expectations you have placed on yourself?

meditation

- Read and ponder these words of Jesus: "Take my yoke upon you. Let me teach you, because I am humble and gentle at heart, and you will find rest for your souls. For my yoke is easy to bear, and the burden I give you is light."

- Consider which responsibilities are essential and which can be let go. Refine your efforts on the responsibilities that God has for you and make changes to eliminate other "yokes" that God does not have for you to carry.

- Write down all of the things that make you laugh and bring you joy. Then write down at least ten ways that you like to have fun or can pursue fun in your life.

chapter 10

discovering the longings of your heart

When we cooperate with our God-given longings for comfort, rest, energy, success, and beauty, we become more fully alive and fruitful in life. God wants to give you the desires of your heart...not just because He loves you, but because He likes you!

As girls, we are very good at getting what we want. My desires are based on my personal perception of what will bring me pleasure. They are powerful because they motivate me in the decisions I make. The more I realize the power of my longings, the more I want them to be healthy, beneficial, and loving.

Just this morning I was having a heart-to-heart with a woman who confessed with tears in her eyes her desire for a man other than her husband. She hadn't acted on it, but the "desire" alone scared her to death. She was smart to get the secret out in the open by telling me, but that's only the first step. Now she has to realize that she is having this desire because of something she believes in her heart. I told her point-blank, "You desire him because you believe in your heart that being with him would bring you massive amounts of pleasure."

"Absolutely!" she said, "I'm convinced that being with him would be a dream come true." What she's beginning to realize, just like I had to when I had an affair, is that an inappropriate relationship – as irresistible, mysterious, and intriguing as it seems – will actually result in *extreme pain*.

It will take work to change a wrong belief in her heart and combat the lie she is believing. Instead of living by default and going with her immediate desire, she is choosing not to follow a desire that will lead her to make a life-altering and destructive mistake. The question is, "How do I get rid of the desire? How do I change something I believe with all my heart?"

Today she *confided* in someone and *owned* the reality of the destructive desire. Now she has to decipher between facts and truth. The fact is…she could sleep with this guy and have a secret relationship him. It would make her feel alive and give her ecstasy-pleasure *for a season of time*. The truth is…that road is actually sabotaged with massive amounts of pain that will most likely lead to disappointment, depression, and broken and irreparable relationships. In essence, this "fun" seems like it's free; it's not costing anything. The truth is that it will cost her more than she could even imagine and she will most likely end up with virtually nothing – no husband, no boyfriend, broken relationships with her children that mean the most to her, and years of her life stolen from her that will take her away from fulfilling her life's dream. Sounds like a pretty big bummer to me. I've walked down this road before and so have countless other women.

My friend believes a lie in her heart. Thankfully she can do something about it before it's too late. But what set her up? How did she become vulnerable to this inappropriate relationship in the first place? Just like me ten years ago, her heart is empty and longing to be satisfied.

The purpose of this last chapter is to help you tap into the desires of your heart that are being left unmet, and help you determine how to fill your heart with answers, solutions, satisfied desires, and climatic-pleasure.

You don't need to be afraid of your own desires. Just seek to have your desires line up with God's because you are safe with Him. He created desire. He can certainly find a perfect match for you! He wants to benefit your life without crossing lines that will bring harm to you. He doesn't want you to live a fake life where you're just obeying the rules and ignoring what's deep inside. He created you to be amazing and free from inhibitions!

Let's see if the longings of your heart are anything like mine.

I LONG FOR COMFORT

If you are craving comfort, don't apologize for it; get yourself some! You deserve to take care of yourself and indulge in activity that brings relief from the pain, anxiety, and distress that accompanies life. All you have to do next is get to know yourself on a whole new level and begin establishing the things in life that bring you the most comfort.

The reason we crave comfort is because we have been hurt, disappointed, and some of us even abused. Where you have your greatest expectations is where you are set up for the greatest disappointment. Most women work too hard and don't receive enough appreciation or acknowledgment.

Sometimes it feels as if no one would really understand how hard we persevere to keep things together and still be emotionally stable. Does anyone have a clue how hard you try to do the right thing and then when you're completely spent you keep on going...and even top it off by stamping a smile on your face?

That's why you crave comfort. This ravenous craving can lead you to a multitude of reactionary substitutes that will put a band-aid on your open sore but never fully heal your wound. Sometimes you crave comfort from the daily grind, other times you get hurt and the craving turn into a desperate cry for help and perspective.

Comfort is not about ignoring or running from problems. We've already talked about the importance of facing the pain and not escaping from it. The kind of comfort that will truly bring us...well, comfort...is what God provides through the Holy Spirit. Jesus called the Holy Spirit our Comforter.[53] His comfort helps us to endure, persevere, and go *through* the situation we find ourselves in.

Comfort from God Himself

I was out doing errands alone one morning when someone did something to hurt me. It felt as if I got stabbed in the back. It wasn't fair and it left me bleeding. I picked up my phone ready to tell someone about this awful and unjust behavior. My mind was racing to decide who I should call, so I asked God, "Who should I tell about what this terrible person did? Bob? My mom? My best friend?" I clearly and instantly heard God's voice in my heart. "I'm enough. You don't need anybody but Me. If you tell any of those people, they will join with you in your offense. They'll be angry at this person who hurt you and they'll have to work through forgiving them. It's okay to share with others sometimes, but we can get through this one, just the two of us."

"Really God? Because I'm pretty mad and hurt. And this person should not have treated me this way. And even though I know you're real, you're invisible. And right now I just need the comfort of a person whom I can see and hear with my own eyes and ears…" I resisted my urge to find comfort my own way. I chose to trust God. I put my phone away. It wasn't easy because I knew I could get someone to side with me and we could talk about the evil offense that took place. I continued my drive to Target talking to God.

I arrived, parked, grabbed a cart, and immediately head-ed straight to the greeting card section of the store. This was strange, because I wasn't there to buy a card. But I bee-lined over there as if my heart was taking the lead on a mission that my head didn't know about. I know it was God. Immediately my eyes zeroed in on one particular greeting card from the sympathy section. The words softly and slowly penetrated the part of my heart that craved comfort. The card said,

> I'm sorry for your loss. That never should have happened to you. My prayer is that you find hope, courage, and understanding during this time.

Tears began to stream down my face. I grabbed the next card. Same thing, just different verbiage. Some of the cards even had Bible verses to bring perspective. I read every single card in the sympathy section. I received comfort straight from God's heart as I cried and heard His voice. I felt loved and cared for.

I received comfort straight from God's heart as I cried and heard His voice. I felt loved and cared for.

Ironically, I clearly remember the God moment in the Target store. But for the life of me, I can't remember who hurt me or what was said. The comfort God gave me that day was so deep and intense that it washed the hurt away and left me satisfied. God has the ability to understand my feelings like no one else. His compassion and kindness caress me because He cares about what happens to me. In the same way, He cares about you, your concerns, the loss, the over-tiredness, and your need to feel comfort.[54]

Comfort Through Little Pleasures of Life

Practical things can *contribute* to your comfort, but your *source* is God. Once that is established, you can allow yourself to search out ways that God wants to fill your need for comfort.

I'm learning not to minimize my own responsibility in finding comfort when I need it. After putting Robert to bed a few weeks ago, I was exhausted from hard work and felt emotionally empty. I knew myself enough to know that I needed some comfort. I had a full half hour to spare (it's amazing what you can do in half an hour!), so instead of just flicking on the TV, I decided on a soothing bath. I stripped down, secured my hair in a headband, and got the bubbles started. I even lit a candle and put on music. The lights were dimmed and I smiled as I slid my feet into the extra-hot water. My feet stung because they are usually cold, but soon my entire body reached the perfect temperature to relax.

What happened next was totally unexpected. Robert apparently was *not* quite asleep and the door wasn't locked. His eyes widened as big as saucers as he abruptly entered the room and accused me, "Oh, so *this* is what happens every night after you put me to bed!" I answered with dripping sarcasm, "Yes Robert. Every night. This is it. Right here. Deal with it. It's all about me. Now get back to bed!"

This whole bath thing may not be appealing to you at all – but it's free and doesn't make you fat! I have some other coping-comforting habits that include high doses of calories and require a budget. Probably my favorite is a full-body massage, but that can become costly. I just got an idea! I need to buy Bob some massage-giving lessons for Christmas. That will solve this issue! However you and I both know that a wife naked on the bed will not merit a full-hour of non-sexual touches. So much for that creative cost-cutter!

Speaking of which, Bob and I recently interviewed Bill and Susie Davis on our daily TV show, *It's A New Day*. Susie recently authored the book, *Uncovered: Revealing the Secrets to a Sexy Marriage*. The four of us taped hours of animated conversation that helped men understand women in the area of intimacy, and helped women understand themselves! When husbands were surveyed on the benefits of making love, many mentioned comfort. Susie and I looked at each other with puzzled looks... really? Comfort? It's an idea to explore; another thing that's free with no calories!

I know some of you aren't married and others of you aren't happily married. I also know that every person craves the kind of relationships that bring comfort and joy. So talking like that may just make you feel unworthy and unbeautiful. That is simply not true. It may appear that a happily married person automatically feels the warmth and comfort of drama-free bliss, but that is never the case. Every marriage takes selfless giving and sacrifice. It's not always roses and daisies. But we cannot depend on our marriage to be our source of value and beauty; it will never satisfy. Yet, relationships with close friends and family bring are key contributors to our comfort. David in the Bible experienced friendship from Jonathan that he described was "deeper than the love of women."[55] We can experience very deep, authentic, healthy love and comfort from close friends. The key is to make sure that God remains our number one source of comfort and we are not relying on friends to give what only God was meant to supply.

Thankfully, the principles of finding comfort aren't hinged on where your relationships are at this moment. And finding comfort for yourself will benefit all of your relationships. A happy single person will be a happy married person. Unfortunately, it goes both ways: an unhappy single person will be an unhappy married person. We often put too much onus on a certain relationship to make us happy. It may sound cliché, but it's the truth: relationship with God is your ultimate source of comfort and joy, and any other great relationships are simply icing on the cake.

Relationship with God is your ultimate source of comfort and joy, and any other great relationships are simply icing on the cake.

Okay, I had to mention cake. Drastically switching gears here, I also find comfort in eating fresh baking from the oven, warm chocolaty drinks, and pretty much carbs, carbs and more carbs. Years ago one of my best friends was having a tough couple of weeks at work. I knew she was in love with my famous Bull Sheet Cake. It's our own special name for Texas Sheet Cake. Chocolate cake made from scratch with thick, creamy, chocolate icing. I baked the cake, filled an ice bucket with ice, grabbed two glasses and a two-liter of Diet Coke. I sat at her desk with her and we ate and drank to our heart's content. I don't recommend this kind of indulgence on a regular basis. But a girl's gotta do what a girl's gotta do once in a while. (The recipe is in the appendix at the end of the book!)

What brings you comfort? Some of my friends like retail therapy. When they need comfort they shop till they drop. For me, I find very little enjoyment in shopping even though I love wearing great clothes and accessories. Weird! We are *all* weird because we are all unique – and celebrating our unique desires is what makes us awesome!

I personally find comfort in talking to a best-girlfriend without any filters, resting in Bob's embrace, pancakes, a good movie, and iced tea. (Not all at the same time!) I also take long walks in nature with headphones listening to really good music and bask in the sunshine. I love getting into bed at night with fresh, clean, crisp, bleached white sheets.

It brings me comfort to be in a comfortable environment that's safe and predictable. Every weekday morning that we are in town Bob and I, Robert, and Winston the dog walk down the street to the school bus stop. Our particular street is full of boys all around the same age, and every single morning there is animated laughter with the other parents as we throw the football and wait for the bus. I can be in my slippers and sweats with obvious bed-head, or dressed up and ready for a meeting.

There are no expectations at the bus stop, and there is definitely no judgment. We laugh together, love each other's kids like our own, and enjoy a comfortable community feeling. I love to be around people where there are no underlying undertones of judgment, and I love going out with no make-up and no care in the world what people think. That environment brings me comfort.

You will have your own list of what gives you the most comfort. As you learn to *like* yourself, you can be creative even if you're short on time or money. There are things custom-designed just for you!

The ultimate comfort is knowing that whatever you do, you are never alone. Be aware of God's constant presence. Call me crazy if you want, but often when I'm driving by myself I clasp my hand and put it the passenger seat just imagining that I'm holding God's hand. I need Him every day. Every moment. All of these other activities can contribute to our comfort, but nothing will ever replace the power of intimate relationship with God. Nothing can satisfy our longing for comfort like being with Him.

about you

- What personally brings you comfort?

- Do you seek wrong comfort from someone or something? What pleasure do you believe you will derive from this destructive behavior?

- God can give you new desires. Are you willing to trust Him to do this? Do you believe that God knows what will bring your true pleasure and comfort?

meditation

Reflect on this verse: "You will make known to me the path of life; In Your presence is fullness of joy; In Your right hand there are pleasures forever."[56]

Meditate on God as your ultimate Comforter.

I LONG FOR REST

Last year right around Christmas, my ankles swelled up like balloons and I could hardly walk. After weeks of trying to figure out what was wrong with me, I finally went to the doctor and was diagnosed with Rheumatoid Arthritis. I quickly found out that it is a chronic disease, something you live with forever. It deteriorates your joints and can even cause crippling and deformity. It was very hard for me to even fathom this diagnosis, for I always have seen myself extremely healthy, lively, and energetic, and presumed I would be a disco-dancing-great-great-grandma fifty years from now!

The first thing I did was remember some teaching and research I had heard about the spiritual roots to sickness. With arthritis, the root negative emotion is bitterness. I couldn't think of a single person that I was holding resentment towards. I needed wisdom and perspective and emailed my mentor and friend, Dr. Jim Richards. In his loving way, he said to forget trying to figure out *why* because that would get me into self-judgment. He said that the key is to live in peace and alkalize your body. Jesus would journey with me to find the root of the problem.

I cried tears of being loved after receiving this news because of the grace that was being extended to me. I don't need to judge myself. Without getting into details, for that would take another book, I learned that our bodies are acidic and alkaline. I needed to stay away from acidic foods to bring balance to my system. I also needed to end my sugar-addiction. So much for chocolate-cake-comfort!

This taught me much about motivation and desires. Yes, I want fresh baking and I enjoy sugar, but I want freedom from pain and disease even more. As I persuaded my heart of that truth, the belief was established in my heart and saying no to sugar became a much easier decision. I am learning to write the truth on my heart: *Healthy food brings me great pleasure and comfort as I feel rejuvenated, energetic, and full of life.* I eat food for pleasure, but also for healing and fueling my body. As I establish the truth of God's principles and freedom, my victory becomes effortless.

Most of my life I have fought my battles by implementing mind over matter using self-control and a strong will. I am astounded at the effectiveness of God's solution to establish His empowering beliefs on my heart. Then I live from the inside out and the battle is won at the very core of who I am.

The arthritic pain subsided very quickly as I radically changed my eating habits. Two months later I visited our close friend, Dr. Don Colbert in Orlando to get his medical advice, mostly to make sure it was a good decision for me to fight this sickness without prescription drugs. His holistic approach in dealing with sickness is to:

- Find out what my body doesn't like
- Check for toxic emotions that have attached themselves to my organs
- Check the strength of my organs
- Discover the supplements that my body is craving

Dr. Colbert didn't find residue of toxic emotions such as shame, grief, and unforgiveness like he did when I saw him a couple years after Robert was born. I breathed a sigh of relief, thankful that I was in touch with the beliefs in my heart, and determined to remove disempowering lies that I hung on to. My check-up was almost complete until he got to my adrenal glands. His eyes rounded and he asked, "How long are you going to be here in Florida?" In other words, *How much time do we have to deal with this – you are a CASE, woman!* Of course he didn't use those words.

He proceeded to tell me that my adrenal glands were shot. I had been living off adrenalin-energy for probably most of my life. He said I was like a Toyota driving with the pedal to the metal, and now it was stuck. I didn't know how to turn it off. I was on a short road to complete burnout. Working too hard, stressed out, and maintaining that big smile on my face the whole time.

I have a tendency towards icy-independence. I'm capable, I can do it, I don't need help, and I won't quit till I'm finished. That's why I call it icy – it's cold! It's well disguised beneath my warm and fun-loving personality, but believe me it's there – just ask Bob! This high level of determination can shut out my dependence on God, and that's where I cross a line and get into huge trouble. There are positive implications with this personality trait; in fact, it's powerfully effective in achieving goals, but it must remain surrendered. And I continually remind myself that I am at my very best when I hand over the reins to my extravagant Father who always knows the ultimate best. Jesus only did what He saw His Father doing. I want to be just like Him.

God spoke to me as I lay awake during a sleepless night a few days later. He told me that I am in a garden-hospital right now for the purpose of rebuilding and resting. I should only do what I have to do. I intentionally identified my cares and cast them toward Him.[57] Just like casting a fishing line, I gave him the things I was worrying about: Our calendar and work schedule, our children and their futures, and all the things that needed to be done. I remembered a song I sang when I was a little girl, the lyrics taken directly from Scripture:

> Consider the lilies, they toil not nor spin. They bask in God's sunshine, they drink in God's rain. If God cares for them in such marvelous ways, how much more, how much more, how much more! Will He care for me, and supply all my needs every day![58]

Just like lilies, you have created for *beauty*, not just *function*. Our culture cultivates and rewards function, which places tremendous expectations on us. The truth is that you are a daughter of the King and you are different because of it. You have a Father who will always provide for you, protect you, promote you, and love you perfectly.

Just like lilies, you have created for beauty, *not just* function.

Jesus is called the Prince of Peace. Through my journey to healing, I have come to a greater understanding of the high priority God places on peace and rest. If we were to have a ladder that measures the things God deems most valuable, I believe peace would be in the top three. The Bible says that "the Kingdom of God is...living a life of goodness and peace and joy in the Holy Spirit."[59] Knowing this settles the question of *stress*. We were not meant to live with it. I'm on a journey of learning more of how this plays out in my life.

I see it like this. My mission is to get from A to B in any given day. I have my list and I have a plan. Because I had been in overdrive, my path looked more like a slinky than a straight path. For every step I took, I ran an extra quick circle. So I was moving fast and hard, but running in circles and taking longer to get from A to B. Now I can accomplish the same amount without frenzy.

Let's talk about you. Do you live with too much stress? Is it affecting your health? Do you live with physical pain, disease and sickness? Let's make something abundantly clear. If you are sick, it doesn't necessarily mean that you have toxic emotions or stress like I did.

John 9 records a question that Jesus was asked: "Why was this man born blind? (Notice that crazy *why* question again) Was it because of his own sins or his parents' sins?" (They *presumed* sickness was because of sin!) Jesus answered, "It was not because of his sins or his parents' sins. This happened so the power of God could be seen in him."[60] The next thing that happened is really cool. The man did what Jesus told him to do and he was healed.

When I found out I had arthritis, I was shocked and confused. *Why me? What did I do wrong? Should I be dealing with toxic emotions in my life? Why aren't you instantly healing me like you did with so many in the Bible?* The man in John 9 did what Jesus told him to do. That's where I'm at today. If Jesus is telling me to lay off the sugar, I'm going to do that. If he has brought a doctor in my life to tell me what supplements are aiding the healing of my body, I will be diligent in taking them.

Let's not stress about analyzing the "why." Let's just do what He is leading and instructing us to do. He wants us healthy and energetic and wants to benefit our lives. I think it is wise to heed to the counsel He brings us!

PRACTICAL WAYS TO REST

Give your body a rest by learning to physically relax and examine your schedule. Give your immune system and digestive system a rest by eating healthy, fasting regularly, and detoxing. Give yourself as much rest at night as possible – your body heals you while sleep.

What does it take for you to get physically relaxed? Whether you have one minute or can spare a few hours, there are practical ways to get lusciously free from stress.

Get out into nature

I find much comfort in the beauty of nature. And even if I don't have immediate access to the bubbling brook and crispy autumn leaves crunching beneath my feet, God gave me the gift of an imagination! I paint a picture in my mind and then I exhale imagining all stress leaving my body. You may be convinced that I'm a crazy-hippie-girl that grew up in the seventies – but try it!

Take a deep breath

If I have a few moments and crave comfort, I simply breathe deeply and meditate on God's peace. As I inhale, I envision myself breathing in God's peace as He leads me to green pastures and still waters. Deep breathing settles your physical body and your mind will quickly follow suit. The best part of relaxing your body and mind is that it opens the door to hear what's in your heart. The heart is where you commune with God. Getting God's perspective in any given moment brings immediate comfort and consolation.

Learn to relax your mind

> But those who wait on the LORD
>
> Shall renew their strength;
>
> They shall mount up with wings like eagles,
>
> They shall run and not be weary,
>
> They shall walk and not faint. [61]

I've loved this Scripture my entire life. This doesn't mean that I sit and wait for God to do something! Jim Richards says, "The word *wait* here means to wrap something around, or bind together. And *renew* means to exchange! When we meditate and wrap ourselves around Him and become *one* with Him, we *exchange* strength. We experience His strength instead of our own strength."

Our minds are busy, busy, busy. We have an opinion about everything and presume the outcome of any given situation based on past experiences. When something happens, we don't tend to consider or ponder what God's opinion is, we already have one! And we interpret the situation in light of our opinion! Oh, if only we could stop and form an opinion based on what God says. Life would be so much different! We could live a life full of faith!

How do we relax our minds? Just visit any health store and you will find supplements and products to help you detox your kidneys, your colon, your liver, and probably countless others. Have you ever considered detoxing your brain? What? Set apart a period of time and fast (abstain) from being introspective and analyzing. As soon as your mind begins to scrutinize and dissect relationships and you're tempted to investigate the "why" to all the questions in your head, cast your care to God and ask Him to take care of it. Then choose to listen to His opinion. Our minds are amazing and active, but I think they deserve a break once in awhile!

I took on this challenge and found it brought me to new levels of freedom. In conversations with God, I found myself listening to Him more and hearing His perspective. Probably because I finally stopped talking! Wouldn't you know, challenges arose – big surprise! The week I did this, my period came nine days early. I know this sounds frivolous, but that had never happened to me before. Questions immediately arose in my head: Am I entering into menopause? How could this have happened? Is this normal? I need to Google this and get to the bottom of it!

Instead I stopped myself and thanked God for His opinion. Instead of worrying about it, I stopped and thanked God for the four children I gave birth to, and hey, if I'm entering into the next season, so be it! No analyzing. No Googling. Then one of my kids went through a life-altering crisis. All during the week I was "fasting" from analyzing. Instead of freaking out, I thanked God for His wisdom and perfect solution.

This all happened months ago. My kids are all just fine and I haven't had a "late" period since. What good would my hours of worrying and fear have accomplished? Does worrying about it add one single day?[62] Let's do ourselves a big favor and challenge ourselves to stop over analyzing and getting overly introspective. It can zap the joy right out of us and it blocks us from enjoying the peace of God and trusting Him relentlessly.

Refuse to blame

Probably the most effective way to find rest in the deepest places of our heart is to refuse to blame the people and circumstances around you. Blaming is avoiding the matter at hand completely. Imagine that you have been given a mallet to crush a cluster of grapes to begin making wine. As you begin, you look like a blind person because you're pounding two feet away from the grapes like a maniac, destroying everything you can, but leaving the grapes untouched. That's how we are.

God longs to take our difficult challenges and make our life like robust and smooth wine, but instead of partnering with Him and crushing the grapes, we go about crushing everything else.

We would love to crush and punish the ones who have hurt and abused us. But it won't do any good at all. It makes us blind fools. In fact, as long as you are blaming a certain person or your situation, you will not see victory in your life. Change is inevitable, but growth is optional. Take a rest from blaming and courageously pursue the places in your heart where you can be transformed.

Change is inevitable, but growth is optional. Take a rest from blaming and courageously pursue the places in your heart where you can be transformed.

The questions most asked of us are, "Bob, how did you actually forgive Audrey after the affair? How did you let it go and begin enjoying life again?" and "Audrey, how do you keep telling your story and not get overcome with shame and regret for what you did?" The reason people ask these is because most people are stuck in their unforgiveness and shame. It is limiting their life and stealing their joy. They want the magic answer.

It may not be betrayal in marriage, but all of us live in a broken world with fragile relationships. Forgiveness must become a lifestyle. Trying harder isn't the answer. That may actually prolong your healing process. However, finding Jesus on a deeper level can catapult you to the life you've always dreamed of. Knowing you are loved by Him, where you listen to His voice and thrive in your secret place, will give you courage. We forgive because we have been forgiven. We love because we have been loved. Forgiving others is a gift we give ourselves. When we like ourselves, we choose to live free of resentment.

I smile more when I don't analyze and refuse to blame others and carry regret. It's a journey to healing, and some circumstances have taken me months and years to get through. But I find myself more thankful. I live easily, freely, and uninhibited in my thought life, not bound by bitterness and introspection. It's easy to like myself when I'm not judging myself constantly and participating in negative self-talk. I have more peace than I ever have before.

Isaiah 26:3 says, "You will keep in perfect peace all who trust in you, all whose thoughts are fixed on you!" I realize that living in peace feels impossible when you're surrounded by threatening situations. It's in these times we have to remember the valuable resource of our imagination. God gave us such a gift when He gave us our imagination! We can reflect and visualize all the times God has answered our prayer in the past and think, *If He did it before, He can do it again!* We can imagine the end from the beginning and see Him working on our behalf. It's in this place that we are forming the future that is in agreement with His promises.

Learn to stop fixing people

I don't think we really know the extent to which we do this, but usually as women we want everyone around us fixed and happy. If they're not fixing the problems themselves, we "encourage" them. There's nothing wrong with being a cheerleader and offering God's perspective, but we cross the line when we obsess about another instead of trusting God and fighting for them in the place of prayer.

Praying for the ones we love is thanking God that He loves them, is caring for them and leading them. Praying for the ones we love is seeing the end from the beginning, thanking God that they are healed, whole, free from addictions, and receiving unconditional love. Praying for the ones we love is NOT controlling the process. We somehow think that we need to involve ourselves in answering God's prayer…but do we really trust Him?

I got a crash course on this about two years after Robert was born. On the outside our marriage was going fairly well, but I knew that life was different because of my affair. Where we used to laugh and have fun, our home was clouded by Bob's anger and depression. He managed to be kind, but I could tell that he was depressed and I blamed myself. In order to compensate for my mistake, I took full responsibility to earn back Bob's love and do everything earthly possible to make him happy. Unfortunately for me, nothing was working.

I was horribly fatigued…emotionally, physically and spiritually. When I wasn't cleaning the house to make him happy, I was trying to prove to him in yet another creative way that I loved him and desired him. When I wasn't doing those things, I was fervently praying and begging God to make him "all better." I did everything I knew how to do and the lack of results left me discouraged and drained.

Bob left the house for work this one particular morning and I could see the never-leaving cloud of depression as he mumbled on his way out the door. Desperation gripped me as I said goodbye and grabbed my journal and Bible. I desper-

212 like yourself, love your *life*

ately searched for God's wisdom as I wrote down this question, "How do I live with a depressed man?" I needed to know what God expected of me because I was completely worn out and had nothing left to give.

The Lord in His faithfulness and comfort heard the cry of my heart and answered me, "Changing Bob is not your job." The answer may sound too simple, but it was profound for me because it came straight from God's heart. I asked God to forgive me for believing the lie that since I was the reason for his depression, then I must be the one to fix him. God reassured me it was time to stop trying so hard and surrender Bob in full trust to my heavenly Father. It was like a weight lifted off me.

God spoke to my heart that it was definitely a new day and it was time to turn a corner. Instead of spending my entire day trying to think of how to make Bob happier and begging God to fix him, God invited me to enter a season of preparation, like Queen Esther preparing to meet the king. I heard the words, "Audrey, it's going to be all about you and me and our relationship together. I want to make you whole, and I'm going to make you irresistible to Bob." I quickly found out that the most irresistible thing to a man is a woman who is *not* trying to change or fix him. Even though Bob didn't hear details about this God-encounter until years later, I clearly saw how important it was that my own heart was transformed, and then God moved on Bob's life. I trusted God deeper and the Lord met me in my pain and gave me practical steps to turn my turmoil into triumph. True rest is trusting God to take of care of the people around you.

about you

- How would you describe your stress level? Are you determined and capable to do it all? In a paragraph written to God, admit your need for Him.

- In your thoughts, do you blame others for your problems? When you stop blaming, you can pursue healing for your own heart.

- Are you on a mission to fix anyone in your life? Write down a prayer of trusting God for that person. Repeat it as often as you think of them.

meditation

- God has rest for you. Read these verses and ask God to help you enter into His rest.

  God's promise of entering his rest still stands, so we ought to tremble with fear that some of you might fail to experience it. For this good news— that God has prepared this rest—has been announced to us just as it was to them. But it did them no good because they didn't share the faith of those who listened to God. For only we who believe can enter his rest...

So God's rest is there for people to enter, but those who first heard this good news failed to enter because they disobeyed God. So God set another time for entering his rest, and that time is today…So there is a special rest still waiting for the people of God. For all who have entered into God's rest have rested from their labors, just as God did after creating the world. So let us do our best to enter that rest.[63]

I LONG TO DANCE

As God heals your heart, and you begin to find rest and comfort and actually forgive yourself, your newfound freedom will light a fire in you. Where you have had pain, you will have passion to help others. Tap into someone's passion and bam! You'll discover an energy source that's unstoppable. If you're lacking energy and praying for some motion-potion, specify your prayers, and ask God for *passion*. Passion is intense, over-powering emotion with keen enthusiasm that will fuel an un-forgettable adventure.

Purpose collides with *passion* when you establish why you were created. The Bible says that we are Christ's bride and His ambassadors.[64] As a daughter of the King of kings, you are beautiful and highly favored. You are in His care and custody. Each day is a gift to unwrap as you embark on an adventure of trusting Him, obeying Him, and seizing the opportunities that nurture the flow of life.

Rest and comfort must marry risk and adventure. When I betrayed my husband, I was overtired and in desperate need of comfort. But I was also living the mundane and longed to involve myself in something impossible – a pursuit bigger than myself. I was busy and bored all at the same time. We are created to abandon rest and comfort for seasons of time, embrace our nobility as princess warriors, and embark on quests designed by God to change the world.

This does not mean we quit our day jobs, take a break from the daily responsibilities as moms and wives and join the CIA. In fact, it has very little to do with what goes on in our outside world. Seeking adventure and playing out our passion has mostly to do with the invisible world.

My sister-in-law Lisa and I love to talk about our relationship with God and the intriguing conversations we have with Him in our secret place. I remember taking a walk with her and she got animated and said, "The world we see with these eyes isn't AS REAL as the invisible world that is we see with our eyes of faith! It's as if there is a zipper in front of us and we can just open it up and see what's really going on!" We laughed as our conversation ignited passion and then decided we'd be "zipper sisters."

Rest and comfort must marry risk and adventure.

I live in the most holy place, my secret place in the depths of my heart. I bask in God's presence, I feast at His table, and

I drink the wine of God's pleasure and joy. I engage in battles, sacrifice comfort, and fight for my King. I remain in His peace and I revel in His extravagant love. It may look to *everyone else* that I live in Phoenix, Arizona, but I know the real truth!

A few years ago I was driving alone to church on a Wednesday evening when something very unexpected took place. I was expressing love and devotion to God, getting kind of lost in His presence, very aware of how real He was to me. An awe of very holy and divine reverence came over me, a sober realization that I was in the presence of an extremely important King. I heard Him speak in the quiet place of my heart: "I delight in you, Audrey, so much so that I want to give you anything you want – up to half My kingdom." I remembered the story in the Bible where the young girl danced before the king, and he was so immensely pleased that he made her the same offer.

I pulled into the church parking lot and sat completely still in my car. I could hardly move as the air was thick. Two worlds collided as I felt the invisible world where I live with God opening up to me in a way I have rarely experienced. I took his question very seriously. What do I want? He's asking me, and I must answer him. I thought about my desires for my future and our children. But only one visualization enraptured my imagination. I saw myself at the gate to heaven one day. As I stood there with Jesus, millions of people poured through the entrance and I knew it was the result of my life. I said it out loud: "Jesus, because of my life here on earth, I want you to use me to break the chains off people that are holding them bondage and in prison. Not thousands, and not tens of thousands… millions."

That is an experience I will never forget. I've thought about it many times since and I've seen God prepare me to display massive amounts of His glory to people who are lost, confused, and need Jesus. I've watched how he's grown my sphere of influence so that I am able to promote Him on levels that I couldn't have created for myself.

In the days that are ahead I want to be vigilant to remove chains off people. What are the chains? Fear of the future; fear of death; fear of being alone; fear of failing; fear of abuse; fear of rejection; pride; trying to look good on the outside; impressing others; guilt and condemnation; fear of having no money; judgment, bitterness, resentment; sickness and disease; deception; wrong identity and sin.

Just like you, God has created me with unique capabilities, talents, and abilities. However, they are only eternally effective as I am surrendered and dependent on Him. As a princess warrior I am influential, uninhibited, and fearless in presenting God's freedom to those in chains. The enemy hates me because of the freedom I promote. He has a scheme to wear me down and get me tired, get my guard down and compromise. He wants me to feel ashamed, stupid, and ineffective. He wants me to hate myself.

Here's the truth: God is with you in this moment to wash you until you are sparkly clean. Pristine. Perfect. Pure and glistening down to the last detail. Find rest in his cleanliness and freedom. You have wonderful adventures ahead and He has plans for you to go much further than your wildest imagination can conceive. When you're alone in your secret place and He asks you want you want, you will have an answer. He is crazy in love with you.

Say Yes To the Dance

My favorite memories take place in the secret place of my heart. A couple of years ago, God surprised me with a question, "Would you like to renovate a room in your heart?" Whenever I think of my heart, I either associate it with a garden or a mansion. Answering this question didn't even take a second, "Of course I would!" This experience just keeps getting better. It wasn't just any room, it was the ballroom. Are you kidding me? I didn't even know there was a ballroom in this mansion, and I love fairytales and princesses and this sounded like a dream come true with a "happily ever after." He showed me the sign on the door to the ballroom that said, "I AM" and then He asked, "Do you trust Me?" Of course I do. I went to sleep that night dreaming of orchestras, flowing gowns, and a perfect moonlit night. I know what people do in a ballroom…they dance.

The next few weeks brought demanding challenges. I soon remembered that whenever you renovate you get rid of what you *don't* want, and *then* begin designing and planning for what you *do* want. The demolition process is not exactly an easy time. In fact it involves breaking things at times. The year before when a group at church was studying David, I was asked to speak on brokenness. And that's exactly what God was doing in my own heart. When you get squeezed, what's there *will* inevitably come out! What I faced head on during this renovation was fear.

Scary things began to happen. Circumstances involving our finances were looking really grim. As the weeks and months went by full of financial stress, I kept hearing His words that first night of the renovation: "Do you trust me?" Every challenge we face can be overcome by a deeper understanding of God's nature and character. God wanted to impart His promise of provision to me. He wanted to heal my God concept and rebuild this ballroom with truth.

My Relationship with Money

Here on earth, my own dad quit his job as a rocket salesman when I was about five years old. From that time on we lived by faith. That meant that every month was a miracle of God's provision. It also meant that we always had to be very careful and frugal. I was never bitter about this, in fact we experienced literal manifestations of God's power as He provided for us and our family was full of passion and adventure. We also had everything we ever needed.

Then I married my husband Bob, a man who had a heart to be a pastor and minister. He possesses the passion of an awesome preaching machine but isn't exactly passionate about making a lot of money! He works hard, he's smart, and he's not driven by the almighty dollar. He loves to help people at any cost. I love my man. So you get the picture of the two main men in my life.

Back to the ballroom, the crunch was on. And the enemy screamed at me: *You won't have a house to raise your kids in! You will never have more than enough! You're in ministry and you'll always have to worry about money!* And it was a cycle in my life. The Holy Spirit is in the business of breaking the cycles of lack. And for the first time, over a period of three months, I turned up the truth, and refused to believe the lies. And then I did an overhaul when it came to presumption. If I really, really, really trust God as my provider, then I can trust that "the Lord will withhold no good thing from those who do what is right."[65]

Who am I to presume that I need to *own* things here on earth? Who am I to presume that my prayers should be answered in a particular way? Who am I to presume that wealth and riches are measured by what I possess here on earth? I am in this world but not *of* this world.[66] That means my entire point of reference has changed. Things in the Kingdom of God are measured on a difference scale![67]

God wants to benefit me and takes pleasure in my prosperity. Therefore, I am going to persuade my heart of this truth: It is not spiritual to be in poverty. God delights in me having wealth. I never have to worry about money. I will never lack the finances to do everything God has purposed for me to do. I can laugh in the face of fear of the future.

The Invitation

The breaking was done, and even though circumstances hadn't changed, my heart experienced transformation. I had peace and I trusted Him on a whole new level, even while living smack dab in the middle of hardship. I watched in awe as God began filling this ballroom with all the details of a dreamy princess story. The ballroom lacked nothing: the orchestra; the inlaid gold; the vast tall ceilings and enormous chandeliers.

He invited me to dance and I experienced God on a new plain. You see, the purpose of the dance really is just one thing: enjoyment, pleasure! It's the perfect picture of unity, divine order, and the beauty of partnering in the rhythm of God. God's purpose for renovation was to bring me to new levels of enjoying Him in an activity where I can't be self-conscious, can't take control, and can't be timid. I had to trust him, understand the foundational steps, and refuse to hesitate. I learned to find strength in His embrace and follow His lead.

Then came a test. In hindsight, I can see it all, but in the middle of the test, I had no idea. My eyes were distracted by two extremely handsome men watching us dance. They were very attractive to me, and I felt a magnetic pull to get closer to see who they were. I was intrigued by them and got closer and closer. Then I saw their names: Fame and Fortune. They weren't *evil* Fame and Fortune, they were *Christian* Fame and Fortune!

The Lord asked, Is that really what you want? Do you want the fame? Do you want big money? Will this give you the security you've been wishing for?

I have a true confession to make. The reason I was attracted to these two is because I love success. Somewhere in my heart I believed that at the top is Fame and Fortune. If I chose to dance with them I could have it all. With deep intention I turned my eyes from them and turned my gaze firmly on the face of my King. I resisted the temptation. I ignored the two men and I danced with my heavenly Father. The dance continued and I smiled with relief as I knew in my heart that Fame and Fortune had little to offer compared to the pleasure and enjoyment of intimate relationship with the King of all kings. He had chosen me to dance, and I chose Him above anything else.

A few months later, temptation lurked again. I recognized them instantly, but this time, instead of ignoring them, I deliberately went right up to them, hoisted my high heel up and gave them a big swift kick! Their exterior was the thinnest material you could imagine. They were totally and completely empty. No substance. They smashed into the tiniest pieces in a second. They were useless, just a façade.

We must recognize any lies that we believe about selfish ambition and greedy gain so that we are well prepared to be well-known, influential, and trusted with great wealth.

Fame and Fortune are not evil within themselves. Even though it appears as if they destroy families, relationships, and entire lives, they simply reveal what's really in someone's heart. Just like getting squeezed, what's really in there will come out when a person encounters riches and fame.

My prayer is that we will recognize any lies that we believe about selfish ambition and greedy gain so that we are well prepared to be well-known, influential, and trusted with great wealth. I know that for my purpose to be fulfilled in this lifetime, it is necessary to have the means and resources to make it happen. I don't have to be scared of success, but rather embrace it as a godly characteristic. Growing up it felt spiritual to have "just enough." I am persuading my heart to the know the truth of God's desire to bless me abundantly and make me fruitful and effective for His kingdom. I can rest in God's provision. That truth runs deep in my heart.

At first I didn't know how important it is to trust when it comes to dancing. My natural response was to trust Fame and Fortune to provide for me. I was wrong about that. Many highly successful ministers "at the top" seem like they have it all. However, unless they are dancing with the King, they are lonely, bored, and unsatisfied. My prayer for you is that you will personally know the thrill of the dance with the very best Lead ever.

To really be the Princess Warrior you were created to be, you must know your Daddy for who He really is: The King of kings. And we must let Him renovate our hearts and give us courage and strength, so that when the war is waging, we will be the first to obey. Someday we will meet Him face to face, and when our eyes meet for the very first time, there will be a twinkle in His eye and a smile on His face. He'll say, "Well done," and then…we'll dance.

about you

- What passions fuel energy in your heart?

- Ask God to give you dreams of adventure for the future. Envision yourself as the princess warrior He created you to be.

meditation

I hope you never lose your sense of wonder,

You get your fill to eat but always keep that hunger,

May you never take one single breath for granted,

God forbid love ever leave you empty handed,

I hope you still feel small
when you stand beside the ocean,

Whenever one door closes I hope one more opens,

Promise me that you'll give faith a fighting chance,

And when you get the choice to sit it out or dance.

I hope you dance....I hope you dance.

I hope you never fear
those mountains in the distance,

Never settle for the path of least resistance

Livin' might mean takin' chances
but they're worth takin',

Lovin' might be a mistake but it's worth makin',

Don't let some hell bent heart leave you bitter,

When you come close to sellin' out reconsider,

Give the heavens above
more than just a passing glance,

And when you get the choice to sit it out or dance.

I hope you dance....I hope you dance.[68]

I LONG FOR SUCCESS

Whatever you think is successful, that is what you will work towards achieving. Often we don't articulate what success looks like to us, which actually is an exercise in defining our personal values. Your idea of success is personal and precious, something to be guarded in your heart, and something you should never apologize for. Most importantly, your idea of success should be defined. As humans we gravitate to what we believe is successful and avoid what we believe failure. My greatest fear is failure. When I fall short of my expectations or what is expected of me, my tendency is to attack my own worth and beat myself up. I don't like being a disappointment. So I punish myself when I am one.

It's been quite a journey for me when it comes to success. I've been through times when I thought it was evil and selfish, and then realized that God uses us successfully for His plan and He wants us to be happy! Success can make you or break you, but the most important thing to know is that you can't worship success, or it will become an idol. You also can't let it be your source of provision or promotion. It can contribute, but never let success be your source. When that truth is established in your heart, I believe you are prepared for all the success God has wired you for. He created you to be successful!

What does success look like? I thought it looked like a big break…you know the time in life when everything randomly comes together and it's happily ever after? I've seen it happen to people. It's almost like winning the lottery. Without effort their book, music, or business takes off; they become highly influential, strong in demand, and rewarded with big money.

I've had seasons in my life when I stress myself out trying to make this big break happen. *Maybe I just need the right publicist? Or publisher? Or maybe a marketing genius will make it happen? Maybe we're not trying hard enough?* I could never control this big break. God knows I tried! I attempted to make it happen. I had my eyes wide open looking for that right door to run through. I wondered if certain relationships would be the networking bridge that would end up being the pot of gold at the end of the rainbow.

Don't get me wrong, most people would describe Bob and me as very successful even as I waited for this big break. We have a pretty full speaking line-up, a national TV show, and an extremely happy family. There's just that one thing missing – the real big break.

I was patiently waiting for a big break…until something happened. God spoke to my heart and said, "Audrey, you're looking for something you already have…" I was staring at the phone in my hand when He said it. "It's as if you've been looking everywhere for your phone. You've been wishing for this phone, dreaming about finding this phone, praying and believing Me for this phone. It's time I told you – it's been in your hand the whole entire time."

The only lie the enemy can get us with is the threat of lack. He attempts to create a need. Guess what? On the night God spoke this to me I decided: *I'm not buying it anymore! I don't need a big break, I don't wish for a huge promotion, I'm not anticipating a life-changing phone call. I don't need it. I don't wish for it; in fact, I've been a little mixed up. The big break is not the miracle*

I've been hoping for. It's a magic wish that has kept me in a place of disappointment!

Journal entry, September 4, 2009

Today I am free. I don't have to make myself write that book that's going to make me famous. I don't have to prove anything to anybody anymore. I have it all. I'm going to say it again – I have it ALL. I am officially ending the quest for the big break. I am complete. My life just got extremely simple. I get to love and celebrate. I can hug my kids freely, laugh in the face of the future, jump on top of my husband and look in his eyes and smile, and anticipate what this beautiful new day will bring.

I have found love. Not only am I complete, but I am completely loved. I love God, I love others, but also I love myself.

So I say to myself, "Audrey, take a deep breath and stop it once and for all. Stop working so hard but never quite enough. Stop being so good, but never the best. Stop attempting to be something you think you were meant to me. It is the carrot in front of the horse. It's been snipped. Bing! Gone." Now I get to run free with Him. The dream of my heart has always been: Draw me unto you, let's run together.[69]

I persuade my heart of this marvelous news. It's done. Jesus looked into my eyes and told me it's finished. I'm forgiven. I'm accepted. There is no more mountain of success – because I really do dwell in the secret place of the Very Most High. It doesn't get higher than that. As His chosen daughter, I am an heir to His kingdom. I can live like royalty! It's here I don't have to prove my importance and fight for self-worth – for that would be looking for something I already have. I have stopped looking, and I have discovered a new level of peace in my heart. I expect nothing less than His highest for my life. As we delight ourselves in Him, He will give us the desires of our heart![70] That is the big break – and it's what we found when we found Him.

I have never had so much peace. Not ever. I'm remembering collapsing on the leather chair with Bob after wrestling with unforgiveness, two years after the affair. I had dealt with shame, but more than that – with failure and I had to forgive myself for that. That was a glorious day I'll never forget.

The epiphany today is of the same magnitude. I feel like I got saved. I have been peeling off layers of this "success" thing for so many years, but now I have actually died to it. I'm experiencing resurrection life. I don't feel impatient. Or driven. Such peace. There was an idol in my garden and it was ugly. It was called: "One Day." One day I'll have it all. One day I'll be recognized for who I really am. One day I'll be discovered by the masses. One day I'll be wealthy.

That idol got rolled off a cliff and is pretty much shattered to bits.

I am freer than I ever thought I could be. I didn't even know I was bound up, but I know now. I don't have to do one more thing to get approval. I'm completely approved by God. I feel like I'm living in the Garden of Eden. This feels a whole lot like the peace of paradise. Naked. Unashamed. At rest.

I was home alone on a hot day when this happened. That swimming pool was right there and I knew nobody could see me so it was safe to express my, let's call it, "newfound freedom." I couldn't help myself, so I peeled off my clothes and smiled and swam my heart out. Some people call it skinny-dipping, I choose to call it chunky-dunking! I thought I was longing for success, but now I get it – I was longing for approval, and it's something I have had all along.

about you

- Reread the last sentence of the previous paragraph. What have you been really longing for? Have you been longing for something you already have?

- How have you trusted God as your Provider? Identify ways that you have taken things into your own hands to provide for your needs.

- Identify areas you have lack. Identify the lies that you believe in the area of money and tell yourself the truth.

- What does success look like to you?

- What do you think success looks like to God?

meditation

- Do you think God is more happy with you or disappointed in you? Begin to persuade your heart of the truth: He sees you just like He sees His Son, Jesus. You are a success because of who you are in Him.

- Will you come in to agreement with God's view and opinion for your life? Would you be willing to see yourself living out the promises of God?

I LONG TO BE BEAUTIFUL

Why did God give us girls an inherent desire to be beautiful? Whether you're a girly-girl princess or a determined tomboy or a never-will-I-wear-make-up nature hippy, there is a desire for you to be beautiful in whatever form you deem beautiful. Unfortunately, few of us ever come to peace with the beauty God gave us and celebrate ourselves exactly how we are. But when we do, the earth shifts and God's smile aligns with ours, and I believe it becomes worship.

Once we come to terms with who we are and thank God for how He made us, our focus switches from us to Him. No longer are we unsatisfied and self-centered. No longer are we driven to be noticed and admired. Along the journey we search for it, we pay for it, we beg for it, and we cry for it. We want to be beautiful and refuse to believe anyone's opinion but our own negative self-judging belief: We don't measure up. Even the most famous and adored celebrity, one whom the world worships, will seldom be at peace with their beauty in their own heart.

I recently spoke to a young girl, twenty-two years old, one who loves God and has the kind of outward beauty that would turn heads and cause car accidents. I asked her if every girl longs to be beautiful. Her answer was quick, "Oh yes. Definitely. I have a goal in my life, something I want to aspire to. One day I hope to go a whole entire day without wishing something was different about me. One day I want to have a heart at peace and rest knowing that I'm beautiful. I don't have to change anything. That will be a glorious day."

This tells me that our culture has an extremely warped perception of beauty and seeks to impose its view on every girl alive. Even though there's nothing wrong with pursuing beauty from the outward sense, these pursuits do not fully satisfy the heart's cry to be beautiful. Eating disorders, sexual addictions, and many other destructive behaviors are related to a perverted attempt to fulfill this persistent and deep human longing to feel beautiful and be beautiful.

Our longing to be beautiful can be fulfilled by God. When we are in intimate relationship with the one who designed and created us in the first place, and we hear Him call us beautiful, we can't help but let our guard down and decide to believe Him. I feel genuinely beautiful before God – mostly because He has forgiven me. Instead of feeling ugly, marred by sin, and hypocritical, something powerful is released when I believe His words to me, "I don't hold your sins against you. I see you as beautiful, clean, pure and lovely."

That's what I want for you. I want you to believe Him when He speaks these words to you. There's nothing more beautiful than that: To accept yourself, stop trying to bring adjustments, and love yourself for who you are because God does. I want to be beautiful and I am attracted to beauty. However, I'm convinced that beauty is much deeper than physical features and a perfect body, and there is a special light to my countenance and twinkle to my eyes that only God can bring.

I implore you to agree with how God feels about you. Your longing to be beautiful can be satisfied in a moment when you stop hating your weaknesses and seeing yourself as He does. Don't wait for the "one day" when you'll accept yourself completely. This is the perfect day to end the battle within yourself and call yourself beautiful. Forgive yourself and love yourself. Say these words, "Thank you God, you created me beautiful…"

Something happens in your heart when you believe you're beautiful. While I was pregnant as a result of the affair, Bob had a very difficult time being nice to me for obvious reasons. I felt anything but beautiful. In the middle of his intense pain, Bob earnestly sought to persuade His heart of things that were true, lovely, and praiseworthy. Even though he didn't have the strength to use words to tell me, there was a popular country song that year that he decided to dedicate to me. Every time it came on the radio, he turned up the volume and looked into my eyes with tears streaming down his face. If it came on during his ride to work, he would dial my phone and hold it up to the car stereo so that I could hear the words. After the song ended, he hung up the phone. We both cried tears of healing each time we heard the song. Even though he couldn't use his own words to express love to his impregnated wife, he did the only thing he had the strength to do. I will never ever stop being the most grateful girl in the world, for my husband to take me back and love me to life.

> *Good morning beautiful how was your night*
> *Mine was wonderful with you by my side*
> *And when I opened my eyes and see your sweet face*
> *It's a good morning beautiful day.*[71]

Believe the Best

You are about to embark on a life without limits where nothing is impossible! You're getting in touch with the real you – the creative you – where you live all of your dreams and fulfill all of your goals. Acknowledging God's presence will profoundly affect your life. The more you base your identity on Jesus, the more your worth soars to its greatest possibilities and takes you to the realm of limitless living!

As long as you are looking at the past you will repeat it. Your imagination is your window to your future! Take the limits off your imagination and you think of what's possible instead of impossible. The first new step is envisioning your future with eyes of faith. The "dream you" if you will! Don't just take a glance, but enjoy the details of who you want to become. Will you come in to agreement with God's view and opinion for your life? Would you be willing to see yourself living out the promises of God? There is an adjustment that will come to your life where you move into agreement with God's preferred future and you begin with a simple, "Yes, I am willing." Then be prepared for the hand of God to touch your life and energize the miraculous within you. This is just the beginning of the new you!

God loves to make things new. We are amazed how He creates order in the midst of chaos and breaths life into what was once dead. From seemingly nothingness He creates beauty. Take us for instance. God had this idea – and it was us – You! After considering every elaborate detail, He smiled as He pondered about "when" He would place you in this world. It would be the perfect time of course. Everything about God is perfect. He knew you long before your conception.[72] Then from His heart of love He gave you His very breath for life. That's the epitome of making something out of nothing!

Now here you are. You have been given this insurmountable gift of life and along the way you've made choices (some better than others). Yet now you find yourself ready for new again. God isn't disappointed in where you are today; in fact, He revels in the opportunity of making something out of your seemingly nothingness. He's a genius at this! He's definitely not holding your mistakes and sins against you, because each one is covered and their penalty paid in full through Jesus. God doesn't just "do" love... He is love.

So here you are…loved. There is a beautiful gift in front of you, begging for you to tear off the exquisite paper and dive into its contents. If you dare to open it, your life will never be the same. It's the gift of new life. If God truly loves making something out of nothing, then maybe, just maybe He can take your failures, your poor choices, and selfish behavior and give you something so wonderful and new that it will exceed your wildest and richest dreams. You are embarking on adventure to release the benefits of your new life. He gives beauty in exchange for ashes. Hope for despair. Peace for confusion. Joy for mourning.[73]

Begin to reacquaint yourself with the essence of this new life. Recapture the beauty, peace, and joy that it holds. Let's not waste another moment wondering if God is here and aware of your circumstances. He knows them full well and continues to yearn to fulfill purpose through you. If you want new bad enough, your heart will hear His voice far beyond the words you read. Deep down you want everything God has prepared for you.

The best part about new is that it simply means, "never seen before." There's life in you ready to be tapped into – limitless, energized, pure, and purposeful life… never seen before. Jesus relates it to a well of rushing waters that never stops. God is capable of invading your seemingly limited world causing his glorious life to flow through you. And that's a calming reality. Once you tap into that daily flow – get ready to live life to it's fullest: effortless, enjoyable, and highly effective.

Happiness is not a golden path – it's a Person. It's your relationship with Jesus. Your happiness is not a reward for making all the right choices. Your happiness is knowing the grace of God to cover you when you fail. Beauty is not "one day" when we finally and miraculously get rid of features we don't like we don't like. Beauty is knowing you are wonderfully made and God is crazy about you. Fulfillment is not finding that missing piece – its knowing the secret that there's actually nothing missing. When we have HIM we have it all. Being appreciated is not being understood by the masses – but by the assurance that He understands how you feel. He knows every time you sit down or rise up. He knows your thoughts and He will walk through every moment - giving you wisdom.

Being content is not settling and saying, "This is just the way it's going to have to be and I'm going to be ok with it." Contentment is actually loving the way it is because you trust Him. It is noble to accept your "lot in life." It life-giving to embrace your life as a gift.

You Have it All

God is your Daddy in heaven who will always protect, provide, and promote you. Jesus is your Prince of Peace and the Holy Spirit is your ultimate Teacher and Comforter. God is everything you have ever dreamed He would be. He will make you happy. He won't ever leave you. He's crazy-in-love with you and he calls you beautiful. He kisses you with God moments and He assures you that He is more real than the chair you're sitting on.

Your heavenly Father wants to give you the desires of your heart. Let this truth sink in and resonate within you each morning as you wake up:

God doesn't just love you…He likes you!
Since He likes you, live today liking yourself
and loving your life!

about you

- The following is one of the best things you can do if you
want to be your own best friend! Write a letter to yourself
as if you were writing to a best friend you admire and
love. Include the following: Describe her *inner* and
external beauty (be specific); what *personality traits you
enjoy*; her *strengths*; what you *appreciate most* about her;
her *passions, desires, and aspirations*. Don't hold back.
See yourself as God sees you through this exercise.

- Put this letter where you can see it regularly. Read it to
yourself each day as a letter from God Himself. Let Him
kiss you with these words of encouragement each day.

meditation

Every need and craving that you have can be satisfied
by a deeper understanding of God's nature and character.
Thank God for the beauty He has given you, and say *Yes* to
the Dance.

about the author

I WISH I COULD MEET YOU IN PERSON, because we aren't just "like" family, we are family! We have the same Father in heaven, and we are definitely going to dance together in heaven one day.

If you're anything like me, I love seeing family pictures, so I've included ours. Bob is on the top left, and working your way clockwise is Christopher (1986), Janelle (1989), Robert (2001), me (1965), and David (1991), and of course Winston the dog. Keep in touch. I would love to hear from you! Visit our Web site to find out current news, and possibly attend a marriage or women's event in your area. Bob and I also host a daily television show! Tune in at www.mynewday.tv.

www.BobandAudrey.com

 Facebook: Audrey Meisner

Twitter: Audreyfun

audrey's sheet cake

I love this smooth, creamy chocolaty cake. It only takes 20 minutes to bake, and it's a snap to whip up. Plus, I usually have all the ingredients on hand! The ultimate homemade comfort food and there's enough for a crowd. Note: It's *very* important that you use a big pan (jelly roll size, 10.5 x 15.5 x 1 inches).

Preheat oven to 350 degrees.

In a microwave-safe bowl:

   1 cup butter or margarine (2 sticks)

   1 cup water

   ¼ cup unsweetened cocoa

Cook on high for about two minutes, and whisk together.

Pour into large mixing bowl and add:

> 2 cups flour
>
> 2 cups sugar
>
> 1 teaspoon baking soda
>
> ½ teaspoon salt
>
> 2 eggs
>
> ½ cup sour cream

Beat well with an electric mixer.

Pour into greased jelly roll pan.

Bake at 350 degrees for 20 minutes.

While cake is baking, prepare frosting:

In a microwave-safe bowl (I use the same one! You don't need to wash in between):

> ½ cup butter or margarine (1 stick)
>
> ¼ cup cocoa
>
> 1/3 cup milk
>
> 1 teaspoon vanilla

Cook on high for about two minutes, and whisk together.

Pour into large mixing bowl and add:

> 4 1/3 cups icing / confectioners' sugar

Beat until smooth.

Frost cake while warm.

endnotes

1   The Bible. 1 Corinthians 13:13

2   Ephesians 3:18-19

3   See Matthew 22:34-40

4   1 John 4:18

5   Psalm 139:1-18

6   Not only did I receive forgiveness from my husband, but the Bible says that God "has removed our sins as far from us as the east is from the west." Psalm 103:12

7   John 8:32

8   James 4:6 and Proverbs 3:34 says, "God opposes the proud but favors the humble."

9   See Romans 12:2-3

10 See Psalm 23

11 See Romans 8:28, 38-39

12 Romans 8:28, 38-39

13 See Isaiah 64:6

14 Song of Solomon 8:6-7

15 See James 4:6

16 Ephesians 1:23 and 3:17, italics mine

17 Galatians 2:20

18   Ezekiel 26:36

19 Hebrews 12:1

20 See Psalm 139

21 1 John 3:1

22 See 1 Corinthians 2:9 and Isaiah 64:4

23 See Jeremiah 31:3

24 See Psalm 139:1-4

25 John 1:12

26 Philippians 4:4

27 Nehemiah 8:10

28 James 1:2-4

29 Romans 14:17

30 Galatians 5:22

31 The phrase "fail forward" is used by John C. Maxwell in his book, Failing Forward: Turning Mistakes Into Stepping Stones For Success.

32 See Psalm 49:5-7 and Proverbs 11:28

33 See Lamentations 3:22-24

34 Philippians 2:3

35 1 John 4:18

36 See 1 Timothy 6:17

37 See Colossians 2:6-10

38 See Galatians 2:20

39 See Hebrews 12:2

40 See John 8:32

41 See Psalm 23

42 Zephaniah 3:16, The Message

43 NIV © 2010

44 Some biblical examples include Deuteronomy 6:2, Proverbs 10:4; Proverbs 14:23.

45 See James 2:14-26

46 See John 5:19

47 See Luke 10:38-42

48 Psalm 103 outlines many of the benefits that God wants us to remember and receive.

49 Anastasia, 1997

50 Philippians 4:8-9

51 See Philippians 4:4-7

52 "Best Day Ever" by Andy Paley and Tom Kenny. © Song/ATV Music Publishing LLC.

53 The KJV uses the word Comforter, and is also translated Helper, Advocate, Encourager, and Counselor. See John 14:6; 15:26; and 16:7.

54 See 1 Peter 5:7

55 2 Samuel 1:26. Also see 1 Samuel 18:3; 20:17.

56 Psalm 16:11, NASB

57 See 1 Peter 5:7

58 See Matthew 6:28 and Luke 12:27

59 Romans 14:17

60 John 9:2-3

61 Isaiah 40:31, NKJV

62 See Luke 12:25

63 Hebrews 4:1-3, 6-7, 9-11

64 See Revelation 19:7 and 2 Corinthians 5:20

65 Psalm 84:11

66 See John 17:16

67 See John 18:36

68 "I Hope You Dance" written by Tia Sillers and Mark Sanders, sung by Lee
    Ann Womack. Copyright © 2000, Uni/Mca Nashville.

69 See Song of Solomon 1:4

70 See Psalm 37:4

71 "Good Morning Beautiful" by Zack Lyle and Todd Cerney, © 2000
    Mighty Moe Music LLC, Life of the Record Music, Inc. (ASCAP, Seven
    International (ASCAP)

72 See Ephesians 1:4

73 See Isaiah 61:3

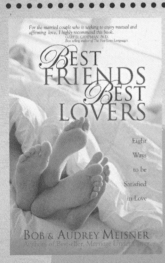

Please visit
www.truepotentialmedia.com/meisner for a free copy of
Bob and Audrey Meisner's, Your Supernatural Marriage
in e-book format.